•THE 2ND LIST
•OF SHIT
•THAT MADE
•ME A
•FEMINIST

Farida D.

Farida D. is an Arab gender researcher and poet, studying Arab women's everyday oppressions for over a decade. Through the process, she broke up with her hijab and set all of her high heels on fire. Farida has been interviewed by BBC Radio London. Her poems are strolling all over social media, and have been shared by renowned artists including Janne Robinson, Willow Smith, and Nathalie Emmanuel. She may be reached for correspondence at: farida-d@outlook.com, or on Instagram at: @farida.d.author

The author is not affiliated or sponsored by the brands, products, or persons mentioned in this book. The author does not condone any acts of violence and any such reference on her part is to be taken as metaphorical not literal.

"Farida is one of the bravest women I have met and one of my favourite writers (truly). Her writing is sharp, funny, honest and painfully needed by this world."

- Janne Robinson,
author of *This Is For The Women Who Don't Give A Fuck*,
and CEO of *This is For the Women.*

To: The girl, I used to be.
From: The woman, I have become.

201.

I am the woman
I wanted to be-
and no one can take that
away from me.

202.

When I was a little girl
I told my father
that I wrote a poem.
"That's wonderful!" he said
"why don't you read it to me
at story time in bed?"

So I read him the poem I wrote
about witches dressed as whores
about virgins who strip for the moonlight
about women who hide under black niqabs
to meet their lovers, as anonymous as night.

I read him the poem I wrote
about girls who become women
who attest
that the best ever sex
is the one they have with their fingers,
about women who have sex for pleasure
not to be mothers,
and about women who chose other women instead of men
to call lovers.

I read him the poem I wrote
about girls who become women
who don't want a prince
or a white dress
or a picket fence,
about women who don't want romance-
instead they want to roam
the world

and leave footprints
in the shape and size of their influence.

When I finished reading
to my father,
his mouth gaped
I could hear the sound of his heart
break
in his chest.
And through a tear drop forming
a familiar pain,
“that’s wonderful” he said
“but please, my girl,
do not write again”.

That’s when I understood
there are different ways
of being free-
and I wasn’t doing
the right one for me.
I could learn, and read, and write poetry
but not on subjects
that men would disagree
with.
For girls and women could only be free,
so long as their freedom
does not disrupt
the patriarchy.

That night I dropped my pen
promised my father
to never write again
but what he doesn’t know

is that instead of writing
I became the star of the show-
living in the world I have once written,
living in the world of brave women.

203.

If the oceans
and mountains
can take space,
then so can I.

If the trees
and their branches
can take space,
then so can I.

If the birds
have no limits
but the sky,
then so can I.

If the men in suits
can take whatever suits
them,
then so can I.

I birthed those oceans and mountains
and trees and birds,
and the men in suits
who pretend they never heard,
of me.

If my creations
can take space,
then this entire world
is my place.

If they live
as if,
they will never die,
then so can I.

***

All life
is born from
a woman.

All life
is ultimately,
a woman.

204.

They tell me
two women
are equal,
to one man.

They tell me
I am just half
of what one man,
is worth.

How?
When he exists, as one,
because I am the one,
who gave him,
birth?

***

What if I was born
from the womb
of a man?

Would I see him,
as a less than?

N.B. In many Arab countries, you need the testimony of two women to equal the testimony of one man in court. A female also inherits half of what her brother inherits.

205.

For centuries
I've been at war
with
men.

Men
whose blood
bled
from the red
wine of my womb,
whose flesh
flushed
from the milk of my breasts,
whose pleasure
pulsed
from the honey of my thighs.

For centuries
I've been at war
with
myself.

***

That's why I always
end up
forgiving him,
you see-
man, he is born
from me.

206.

Whenever I express
sentiments of self-love,
as a woman,
I'm accused of being
a 'man-hater'.

As if,
when I love myself,
as a woman,
there is no space left
to love a man.

They don't realize,
when I love myself,
as a woman,
I leave nothing for hate
I go all the way, generously-
loving myself,
it includes
loving the men
ripped
from my womb.

***

Isn't it ironic
that the men
who hate you,
call you
a 'man-hater'?

207.

Can't you see?
When he calls you
man-hater
crazy,
cunt
bitch
slut,
and whatnot,
he's just trying
to shut you up.

Can't you see?
You were groomed
to seek his validation,
that your worth depends
on a man's admiration
of you.
He knows that, too.

That's why when he feels upset
or threatened by you,
he withdraws his approval, by calling you names
to silence you.

Man-hater
crazy,
cunt
bitch
slut-
are a man's way
of saying 'shut up'.

Next time he
calls you crazy or whatever,
don't hide in your shell
like your world just shattered.
Tell him; what's crazy is that he thinks
his validation of you
matters.

And unlearn that it matters.

208.

No, I don't hate men.

I love men.

I love the way their chests carry fire.
I love basking them with my desire.
I love lying down by their side,
like the sky and the sea
where it's not possible to see
where one ends and the other begins.

I don't hate men.

I hate the system that privileges them.
I hate their silence and comfort,
while I don't have a bed.
I hate watching them spend all the benefits,
paid from my own expense.

No, I don't hate men.
I need them-
I need them to see
that I need them to fight with me
and for me,
and for us,
to be free.

209.

The only war
that needs peace
as the weapon-
is the war between
men and women.

210.

He looks at me
with sad eyes
full of demise,
when I read him another feminist poem,
he feels responsible
for his own kind
for all of the men
for all of their misogyny and lies.

But what he fails to realize,
is that because of him
because he has shown me
that a man can be,
loving, and supporting, and fighting for equality-
because of him,
I now hold higher standards
for his own kind
for all of the men,
because of him,
I fight misogyny.

211.

I was sitting in the airplane
next to a strange man,
pretending he's off to an important
business trip, in Japan.

And as if there was some unspoken rule,
(taught only in boys' schools),
or perhaps it was written on my boarding pass,
in a font tightly suppressed-
he immediately claimed ownership
of our shared armrest.

At first, I kept my elbow tucked under my breasts
but after a while,
I thought- fuck him
he already has the window seat, and I got stuck with the aisle.
Plus,
I was recovering,
from the food trolley crashing
straight into my chest-
the least that I deserve
is the freakin' armrest.

So I tried to take a bit of the elbow space
(not all- I just wanted to share),
but he grew a look on his face,
like 'how could you even dare?',
then he got dressed
with shock and distress,
as if I was stealing
something that was his.

He didn't budge,
(not even to adjust his crown).
He huffed and expanded
into a massive vulgar frown.

But underneath that Broadway
show of masculinity
I could see,
the fragility,
of a man trying
not to breakdown-
he's spreading out,
because he's taught that, 'the bigger the better',
size does matter,
on his side of town.

He won't share custody of our armrest,
because he's terrified that
tucking his elbow closer to his body,
will cause him to shrink down.

N.B. As of 2017, 'manspreading' (spreading one's legs excessively when sitting to occupy more than one seat) is banned in Madrid. (Source: campaign #MadridSinManspreading).

212.

Be a man, they said.
So he stopped crying.

Be a man, they said.
So he stopped sighing.

Be a man, they said.
So he stopped feeling.

Be a man, they said.
So he stopped healing.

Be a man, they said.
So he punched a wall instead,
of squealing.

Be a man, they said.
So he stopped wearing pink.

Be a man, they said.
But he suddenly stopped to think....

What does it mean,
to be a man?

N.B. An Australian study found that young men living up to the pressure of being a 'real man', are more likely to have mental health problems, be binge drinkers, and commit acts of violence. (Source: Jesuit Social Services' Men's Project- www.themanbox.org.au).

213.

Did you know?

Men are afraid.

They are so fucking afraid
of feeling.

They cower behind anger and violence
because all their other emotions
are struggling with healing.

Humans are raw bubbles of wild emotion,
a full spectrum of that shit-
but boys are groomed that to be men
they must learn to suppress it.

Men are afraid.

They are afraid of expressing
what they feel as true,
because they've been taught that 'feeling'
is something that women do-
and they are terrified of being
confused with women,
because they know how much
the patriarchy hates women.

214.

A man who fears
being seen as feminine-
is a man who fears
being treated,
the way he treats women.

215.

We need to heal the feminine within us.
We need to hear the feminine within us.
Women, and men- all of us.

Her softness, is not weakness.
Her gentleness, is not meekness.

There is power, in softness.
There is power, in gentleness.

We think that being powerful means embodying only the masculine,
so we silence the feminine,
and she does listen
burying herself within,
her light begins to dim.

But look how broken she is-
look how broken one can be,
when they lack the feeling
of empathy.

We are human.
We are emotion,
rolled under skin.
We are instinctively expressively chaotic.

The masculine thinks that power,
is aspiring to be robotic.

Who else can see?
The masculine is wounded from rejections

that won't let him be,
a human, free to feel freely.

Power, is not burying your feelings within.
Power is when you empower,
your feminine.

216.

I love a man
when he walks tall
in his feminine.

I love the softness
that knits a nest to nestle
inside his hard
chest.

I love a man
who is so secure
in his masculine,
he isn't threatened
by the embrace
of his feminine.

***

I cannot resist a man
with a well-endowed,
brain-
they say size doesn't matter
but they don't all function
the same.

I cannot resist a man
who measures the size of his girth
and the length,
by the amount of inner
work and healing he's done-
not by his physical strength.

I cannot resist a man
who has ripped,
the privilege off his skin
and studied the oppression
of mine-
a man like that, is just so rare
and so damn fine!

217.

But wait…it works both ways…

Don't you think
there is so much that women
can learn from men?

Look at them!

Not in terms of anger or violence,
but in the way they strip from silence.
Unapologetic, taking up space
like the entire world, is their place.

Look at the way they express
their sexual needs in bed-
I have never heard of a man
too shy to ask for head,
but I know too many women
who are too afraid, they'd fake an orgasm.

Perhaps we can learn
a thing or two, from men.

Don't you think?

218.

And by the way,
women are allowed to be angry
just like men are allowed to cry.

Humans are a wide spectrum of emotion
if we suppress any of it, all our feelings die.

***

But unlike male anger,
which stems, from men,
being taught that anger
is the language, for the masculine to speak-
female anger
stems from being taught
that our feminine is weak.

219.

Our inner feminine
is not weak-
she just needs
healing.

Our inner masculine
is not violent-
he just needs
feeling.

***

To be feminine means to feel,
everything.
To be masculine means to feel,
nothing.

How tragic. How erratic.

How can we embrace our
feminine and masculine,
without being fanatic?

220.

My mother
has a complex relation
with her feminine-
she would paint her lips red
but her tongue spits fire,
she would wear high heels
but walk like a soldier,
it was only when I got older
that I began to realize-
her relation with her feminine
isn't complex-
she is just reconfiguring
patriarchy's mess.

221.

I pride myself
with my career, and earning my own income.
Yet, I discredit (sometimes even loathe),
the work I do at home-
cooking, cleaning, being a mom.

On this road to feminism
women embrace what was traditionally masculine
to achieve equality-
but what about what was traditionally feminine
that no one now wants to be?

Women disdain traditionally feminine roles
men disdain traditionally feminine roles-
we all run after the masculine, and outsource our feminine chores.

We have microwave meals, we hire cleaners, and pay for childcare-
all because men still haven't learned
how to help and share.

It's not a coincidence that nurseries, nannies, and housekeepers
are all jobs dominated by women-
men wouldn't be caught dead doing
a "job meant for a woman".

Housework used to be a woman's job.
Housework must be everyone's job-
and just like women have entered the workforce,
men must also cook and clean, and do other house chores.

On this road to feminism

I struggle to embrace my feminine
because it is shunned as second class.

But if men embrace the feminine, the way women embrace the masculine-
perhaps one day I'll feel proud,
for wiping my baby's ass.

222.

He's angry
because when he came home from work,
the dishes were piling in the sink
and she hadn't cleaned or cooked.

He thinks
he doesn't have to do any housework
because the office has got him overbooked.

He calls her lazy,
because she won't be
his free,
maid-
but how much work would he get done at the office
if he was never getting paid?!

***

Women do not come into life
for a domestic purpose-
to cook, clean, and provide for men
a free household service!

223.

I am a woman
and I do not cook.

But I'll pass down
this recipe for future generations;
I am a woman,
with 0 oz of bone
that senses
how to cure starvation,
0 tbsp of desire
or temptation
to even attempt
a 1 mg flirt with a kitchen's sensation.

I am a woman
and I do not cook.
Fuck you, if that's wrong in your book.

(I eat really well though).

***

A man is never
independent from a woman-
until he can cook and clean for himself.

224.

You are afraid
to love me back,
because I don't need you
to pat my back.

I love you because I *want* you,
not because I *need* you,
as my finance plan-
but boy, are you too stupid to see, through your fragile masculinity
that this is the truest love
a woman can give to a man.

***

Loving you
makes me want to do
all this super feminine shit
like wearing lipstick
and dresses
that ride up my thighs,
and baking cookies
and strawberry pies.

I don't know why.

Loving you
makes me want to be
super feminine-
perhaps I do it

to compliment
and complete,
your masculine.

225.

What if we taught little girls
that glass slippers
are just metaphors for
glass ceilings?

And that bandages
instead of boys
are more effective
for healing?

What if we taught little girls
that the princess
doesn't need saving?

And that the prince
is just the masculine version
of who she is-
when they unite,
all parts of her, are embracing?

226.

Re-interpreting Shakespeare:

All the gender roles are a stage,
and all the men and women;
merely players.

***

You are not born into gender-
you are born into genitalia.

And then,
you are groomed into a gender,
conditioned upon your genitalia.

N.B. Estimates suggest that about 1 in 100 people born in the U.S. are intersex. (Source: www.plannedparenthood.org).

227.

Femininity is a performance.

A role that we decide to play-
no one is born obedient
to what society has to say.
You learn those things, along the way.

Stop and reflect, on the things women do,
to express femininity,
it is merely a role that society
offered you-
are you auditioning?

Or have you been playing
this role for so long,
that you no longer
realize, it's all conditioning?

You paint makeup on for your role
you put on that skin tight skirt, or that uncomfortable baby doll.
Corset and heels
and other sex appeals-
designed to make you attractive
through feeling pain.
Do you see that game?

It's designed to make you associate
that being feminine, is being sexy
and that being sexy is painful-
your sexual being is painful.
If you want to be appealing, you must be suffering and aching-

it's telling you that your feelings,
don't matter.
In this role you play,
you are just designed for male pleasure.

You're not expected to enjoy this role that you do-
but if you do,
you are slut shamed!
Because in this role, you are; sexualized, commodified, objectified
but not allowed to feel *sexual*
or to reclaim,
your body.

In this role you are given,
you cannot win,
either way.
Do you still think
it's all just
fun and play?
Do you still think
you'll get to be,
the star of the show,
someday?

Femininity is a performance.
A role to play a script exactly as it is written.

Femininity is a performance.
And you don't have to audition.

228.

Give yourself permission,
to ditch your
lipstick and heels.
There's no guidebook,
on how femininity feels.

***

He told her
to get a boob job,
that she doesn't look feminine in her flat chest.

She told him
that femininity isn't measured,
by his preferred size of breasts.

N.B. In 2018 alone, Americans spent more than $2 billion on silicone gel breast implants and injectables. (Source: American Society for Aesthetic Plastic Surgery- ASAPS).

229.

I used to hate pink
and flowers
and frilly skirts
and how I blushed
when boys would flirt.

I used to hate softness
and gentleness
and the idea of being
a stay-at-home mom.

And my period
and my weakness
when my cramps
shot like a gun.

I used to hate being girly
and anything
associated with womanhood.

I painfully misunderstood,
what feminism
was about-
I thought I had to bury my feminine
so the world can hear me shout.

How wrong was I.

How much hate was eating me.

The feminine does not discredit me

I don't need the masculine to validate me.

It's time to unlearn-
all those years I internalized,
my misogyny.

230.

Can't you see?

You weren't born self-hating.

Can't you see?

You've been conditioned to think like the men,
you've internalized
their misogyny.

***

If you cannot see,
the misogyny-
it's because you've internalized it so well.

231.

I am not ashamed
of my womanhood,
of the hairs that grow all over my skin
including my vulva, and within.

I am not ashamed
of the blood that peels
the layers of my womb.

I am not ashamed
of the honey that blooms,
from the hive between my thighs.

I am not ashamed
of my breasts, or their size,
or their milk that waters new life.

I am not ashamed of my strife.

I am not ashamed
of my womanhood,
perhaps you misunderstood
the things that I do-
I paint my face, and shave my legs
not because
I hate myself,
I *hide* myself
from you.
You don't get the privilege to see
the real me,
until I completely

trust you.

I am not ashamed
of my womanhood,
and you wouldn't be ashamed
of my womanhood if you were wise enough-
you won't ask me to be more, or to be less
you would take my womanhood as it is,
with acceptance and pure love.

232.

Accepting your uniqueness,
in a world that strives
for uniformity-
is a revolution.

233.

I began to grow my bodily hair
it started out as just a dare
against the judgemental glare,
of my Gillette Venus-
telling me that I can't have a hairy body
because I don't have a penis.

"Says who?"
I said,
"Not me, the men you take to bed"
it replied,
and I realized, the razor was right-
perhaps I need to be prickly picky
about who I let inside,
my cactus.
Perhaps I don't need to shave my body, instead,
perhaps I need to shave fuckboys and their misogyny
right out of my bed.

***

Re-interpretation of Little Miss Muffet:

Little Ms. Pubic Hair,
sat in our underwear
protecting our vulvas each day.

Along came razors
wax and electric shavers,
and frightened Ms. Pubic hair away.

N.B. A hair removal survey conducted by American Laser Centers, showed that women spend up to $23,000 on hair removal in their lifetime, and remove unwanted body hair for an average period of 53.6 years.

234.

"I'm going through a dry spell"

"My virginity is growing back"

Those are the things you say
when you haven't had sex
in a while.
Feeling like there's something wrong
with you,
or with your lifestyle.

But your body isn't designed
just for sex-
listen to it, let it lead.
It will tell you when, and when not,
to have sex,
and exactly what else it needs.

N.B. Dry spells occur, even while you're in a relationship, and it's totally normal. A healthy sex drive is different for each person.

235.

When was the last time
you told your
vulva
that you love her?

Not just with words
with actions.

When was the last time
you let her grow
wild untamed?
Listened to her stories
about being shamed?

When was the last time
you let her breathe?
No vaginal wash or douche or panties or sanitary pads,
or other suffocations that make her go mad?

Have you ever
let a man taste her, raw?
Have you ever
realized, she doesn't have to
taste like a rainbow?

When was the last time
you touched her with love?
Do you realize that
the hands of lovers, are not enough?
She needs you,
too

to feel her spasm.
Do you realize that
you never have to force her
to fake an orgasm?

Do you realize that you
don't have to cater her to the desire,
of fuckboys
who don't understand that vulvas get thrush and perspire,
and infections that burn like wildfire?
Vulvas don't naturally look like a thornless rose,
or taste like candy-floss-
let her educate men on what a vulva is
for the sake of all of us.

Love your vulva
and set her free;
free from commercialization
free from expectations
free from misogyny.

Love your vulva
and let the world see
what a real vulva
looks like,
feels like,
tastes like.

Love your vulva. And try to at least see,
that the way to love her,
is to just let her
be.

236.

When I was a teen, in the good old days,
sanitary pads were so massive
that if the box didn't say
they were for menstruation, without hesitation,
you'd think they were shields for war.
When you wear them, you can't go out,
because it's impossible to pass through the door.

I loved those pads.

If I had three wishes from a genie-
I'd choose three of those pads
over three Lamborghinis.

Today, sanitary pads are designed
so ultra thin, so tiny
so that the men cannot see,
that there's a pad playing catch with blood
inside your panties.

Although they promise to be better-
super absorbent,
and won't stain your knickers,
you still need to be consoled-
for a pack of these every month of your life
will cost you a ton of gold.

And they come scented, of course-
because why wouldn't you
want to smell like
lavender seeps from your pores?

Some even come with wings,
so that you can fly...
...up high
...and far away, in the sky
from men who can't bear to see period blood,
because it makes them cry.

Those companies think that if you can't feel the pad,
perhaps you'll forget you're on your period too,
like their advertisements promise you-
you'll go on roller coasters, wear white,
and might even bleed a Gatorade blue!

What those companies don't know
is that we don't want to go cycling or swimming during menstruation-
we just want to lie down on the couch, and eat chocolate
without moderation.

Those companies don't know that pads aren't just to contain
Mother Nature's monthly assassination-
pads are supposed to be
massively puffy,
like white clouds, fluffy,
like a hotel bed, for a vaginal vacation.

We don't need smaller pads- we need male education,
awareness information
to break that masculine fragility;
periods are super powers-
we don't need cloaks of invisibility.

237.

I pulled out my blood sucked tampon
after hiding in my vagina-
like that old magic trick
where the magician pulls the rabbit,
out of a hat.

He looks at me with disgust
and says:
What the hell is that?!

That- my dear fuckboy,
is how your mother
turned you from seed to human,
and it is extremely, painfully tragic-
that you're repulsed by the blood swimming around your bone
and on my tampon,
instead of seeing it as magic.

238.

Woman
creates life
out of the blood
that lives between her thighs.

Man
creates death
out of the blood
that splatters on his battlegrounds.

The tragedy?

We call
her blood dirty,
and praise his blood
as victory.

***

I've had enough!

If you tell me, one more time,
that my period is dirty,
I won't just tell you,
to fuck off.

I will smear it all over your face-
to remind you what
you're made of.

N.B. Menstrual blood is no less sanitary than other types of human blood. (Source: Science).

239.

How come
human limbs
have a different meaning
when they're put together
to form
a female?

***

I am a woman
broken
into body parts-
into breasts
into vagina
into legs.

Each part, alone, is worth more
than the sum of my whole.

240.

I was happy
in this skin
before you taught me
to cross my legs
before crossing
the doorway
between home and the world.

I was happy
in these organs
before you sent your troops
to invade
and dictate what my parts must do:
breasts for sex
vagina for sex
mouth for sex
legs for sex
hands for sex
sex for sex.

I was happy
in this body
before you turned it into a project
of arts and crafts
for boys who think they are men
and drew the dotted lines all over me,
for them to
...tear here......tear here...
...tear here......tear here......tear here...
...tear here......tear here......tear here......tear here...

I was happy
before you taught me shame and victim blame and doubted my sanity as me being insane.

I was happy
before you.

241.

Stop looking at me
like I owe you
like I haven't paid my rent-
I don't live in the male gaze,
and you don't own my consent.

***

This female body I wear,
this soft skin, this long hair-
the way you gaze at it,
fuckboy,
you make me hate it.

***

We see women,
as objects created for men,
even the woman herself
often cannot see herself,
outside of male eyes-
she judges, shames, and victim blames,
with the misogyny she's internalized.

242.

You are not born
hating your body
no baby ever complains
about not being thin enough
pretty enough
good enough-
you learn those things
when you're old enough
somewhere along the road.

When I was a child
I used to wander
about my body's wonder
this special vessel, that I hide under-
fascinated at how my legs
can make me walk,
how my tongue
can make me talk,
how my round belly
can hold all the food I love,
how my hands can pick up stuff
how I can open my eyes and see
myself in the mirror looking back at me.
That girl can rule the world, with the way she danced and twirled
the mirror praised her, and I would agree.

Somewhere along the road
I started to see
my body, myself, so differently.

I don't remember exactly

when it began
but suddenly
when I look at me
all that I can
see, is self-hatred and hostility;
my cellulite is
like orange peel,
my bum is the size
of a Ferris wheel,
my hips and tits
have no sex appeal,
my stretch marks are
impossible to conceal,
my stomach rolls, from the
guilty pleasure of one too many Happy Meals.
I shave the hair growing between my thighs
because it's not at all ideal,
I clip extensions on my head
fake hair that makes me look real.
Those layers of broken skin
that I reside within
making my body
a temple for sin
I'm not good enough, I cannot win.

Somewhere along the road
I learned this shame
and self-blame
and I took for granted, all that this body granted
me, over the years
it planted
love, and I gave it hate-

what used to be a special vessel
was no longer special, no longer great.

243.

My mother used to say to me:

If you finish your beans,
I'll give you those sweets.

If you do your homework,
I'll give you those sweets.

If you listen to your teacher,
I'll give you those sweets.

If you let the doctor check you,
I'll give you those sweets.

If you behave yourself,
I'll give you those sweets.

Then one day, I began to say to myself:

If you get through this day,
I'll give you those sweets.

If you work hard enough,
I'll give you those sweets.

If you pass that test,
I'll give you those sweets.

If you get that bonus,
I'll give you those sweets.

If you get over that fuckboy,
I'll give you those sweets.

That's when I realized-
because I view sweets as a reward,
the antithesis- healthy food-
becomes a punishment to me.
And so, I struggle to stay healthy.

Suddenly I hear myself say to me:

If you eat healthy all day,
I'll give you those sweets.

If you go to the gym,
I'll give you those sweets.

If you drop those extra kilos,
I'll give you those sweets.

My relationship
with food
is skewed,
as either a reward or a punishment.

And I wonder;
what would be the size of my jeans,
if my mother had rewarded me with beans?

244.

On the kitchen counter
he calls to me
and I know that he tastes
even sexier than what my eyes can see.

Dressed dripping in lemon drizzle
or fudge
or sweet salty rocks,
temptation temptation - I cannot stop.

I take him in me
for just one lick,
just one taste,
just one bite.
And I end up devouring lust
all night.

This kind of romance,
it always starts with just a glance
of the eyes;
a moment on the lips,
turns to a memory forever
in my hips
and thighs.

N.B. Binge eating is the most common eating disorder in the United States. (Source: NIDDK- National Institute of Diabetes and Digestive and Kidney Diseases).

245.

My stomach growled
she's hungry
again.
I just fed her a few hours ago
shouldn't she by now know,
the agony I feel
mentally
with every
calorie count?

She doesn't even *need*
the food,
she just *wants*
to store it
in my hips and thighs
and in my self-doubt.

I won't feed her,
she needs to learn
that food is our enemy.

Can't she fucking see?
That the more she ate, the more I get hate
for all the weight
that I carry on top of me.

Can't she fucking see?
She needs to carry a light plate
because the burden of hate,
is too heavy for me.

N.B. Anorexia nervosa is a deadly eating disorder, and is more common in girls and women. (Source: Mayo Clinic).

246.

I don't need to lose weight.

I need to lose the idea,
that I need to lose to weight
to feel pretty, to look great.

247.

I have a bikini
and I have a body
but according to beauty ideals
I don't have a "bikini body".

The "bikini body" phenomenon shows
that a woman's nakedness
is acceptable, only when
she fits a certain dimension
pleasing for the male gaze
whatever he's into nowadays
skinny or curvy,
big boobs, or small butt
or whatever else he defines
as "hot".

Otherwise, if a woman's body does not match
what a man wants to watch
she must be hidden
unseen
not in a bikini- under big baggy jeans.

I say fuck beauty ideals
and misogyny-
I'll wear a bikini if I want to
no matter what size I am
because what a random
fuckboy on the beach thinks of me-
is something that doesn't deserve
one fucking damn.

248.

If they taught you
that the Master makes no mistakes-
then, my darling,
you're a masterpiece.

249.

My mother, when she eats
she doesn't count calories
she counts happiness.

She doesn't care
about the size of her hips
or the size of her plate,
as long as she was happy
with what she ate.

"You are what you eat",
that's what they say-
and from the curve of her smile
to the curve of her thighs,
you could tell that my mother
eats happiness all day.

250.

She ate and she ate,
not because she wanted
to put on, weight
but because she wanted
to put off, men-
she knew that 'fat' repelled them.

She ate and she ate,
and she wore fat as her shield of protection.

And on some level, we all wear shields-
what's yours?
Take a moment of reflection.

***

I paint lipstick
outside my lips
and shade my eyebrows
outside my hairline.

I draw the boundaries
way beyond, my real lines.

Because if you can't see
the real me,
you won't be
able to hurt her.

251.

I paint this cage
I'm in,
with all the colours
of freedom-
a rose pink, a midnight blue
and a wine red, to please you.

I dress this cage
I'm in,
with bondage
of sex appeals-
a tight dress, a corset,
12 inch high heels.

I mould this cage
I'm in,
to satisfy
your desires-
I eat only air, go under the knife
I reinvent this body
like a dawn under fire.

I paint, dress, and mould
this cage I'm in
to attract you-
hoping you'll set me free with your love.
But all you do
is keep me locked in for you, like a show to view,
by constantly saying
I'm not good enough.

252.

Look at the potions
we pour
over our hair and body,
just to smell pretty.

Look at the chemicals
we paint
all over our face
before we head to the city.

Our hair is spilt and burnt
by straighteners
and coloured dye.

A smoke of
dark circles
evaporates with concealer
under our eyes.

Yet we still cannot see....
the beauty myth is a lie.

Hair styling products
are weapons,
of female mass destruction -
do you think it is a coincidence
that hair dryers resemble shotguns?

And let's not even mention the conundrum-
of breast implants

and cancer,
or tampons
and toxic shock syndrome.

All this stuff
we're soaking in,
that burns our skin-
yet we're still alive.

But for how much longer can we thrive?

We are killing ourselves slowly.

Our skin is breaking out
yet we refuse to hear...
our pores silently shout:

You are the ancestor
of the witch they couldn't burn!
It took them years to learn,
how to develop a different,
less obvious way,
to burn you.
And somehow
they got you convinced
to do it to yourself, too.

***

Women must be witches,
you see-
to survive in this world,

what else can we be?

N.B. Did you know that many of the beauty, hair care, and feminine hygiene products are made with toxic chemical ingredients? (Source: Environmental Working Group Skin Deep database/ and Women's Voices for the Earth).

253.

The beauty industry
creates our self-pity;
and then it thrives, and survives
and profits,
from our obsession
with being pretty.

***

Remember:

It's okay to want to be pretty.
It's okay to shave, to groom, to put on makeup, to wear the cute little dress.

It's okay to want to be pretty-
it's not okay for them to attach your worth
to shave, to groom, to put on makeup, to wear the cute little dress.

It's okay to want to be pretty-
it's not okay for them to reduce you to 'pretty'.

254.

You teach me
that my most
important quality
is being
pretty.

And when I use it
for my financial gain
to model
or do sex work
or whatever,
you go insane
and you begin to shame,
and label me:

'Whore', 'slut',
'attention seeker'
and whatnot.

What am I supposed to do?
Sit there, being pretty,
doing nothing,
but wait for you?

***

A woman's beauty is acceptable
when it's passively waiting
for a man to own it.

When a woman owns her beauty
to work for her advantage, she is slut shamed.

***

Don't judge women
who are famous for nothing
other than their looks-
judge the world
for valuing women
only upon their looks.

255.

"Beautiful"
is not the most
important thing
a woman can be.

256.

The beauty industry
creates
our insecurities
and builds empires of solutions,
to sell us promises,
and then profit from our delusions.

Your skin is breaking!
Use this lotion.

Your face is ageing!
Use this potion.

Your hair is falling out
your stomach is rolling out
your this or that...

Stop for a second and think to yourself;
why are those things bad, anyway???

Why shouldn't my skin break?
Why shouldn't I age?
Why must I erase the lines on my body
to look like a blank page???

The beauty industry
creates
our insecurities,
to make fortunes of profit that last long-
those changes in your body are human
those changes in your body aren't wrong.

257.

And they say
wear those hot pants
take that Boudoir shoot
so that when you're older
you will look back
to see how sexy you were.

But darling,
look at you now-
like fine wine
and honey,
with age, they taste better.

Look at the skin,
you've grown in,
how you understand yourself, from within-
you've never been sexier.

258.

Now what?
Now that I've paid all my dues,
wrapped my ribs in a corset
and the anchor of my toes in high heeled shoes.

Now what?
Now that I've obeyed all the rules
the right paint on my face, the right length on my hair, the right dress to wear
the right to not choose.

Now what?
Now that I've changed the way I look,
sucked the fat out of my hips
built it in my butt.

Now what?
Now do you think that I'm hot?
Because I feel cold
replacing my warm skin, with plastic-
all for you to think
"oh wow, she looks fantastic".

Now what?
Now that I am no longer me
I ask you now,
do you love me?
Because I'm trying each day
to love this stranger,
in my mirror,
looking back at me-

trying hard, to find myself
in who you want me to be.

***

I'm judged
for not being beautiful enough,
and judged
for getting cosmetic surgery-
what is this fuckery?

259.

It is not on my limbs
or in the length of my dress.

It is in your eyes, fuckboy-
your eyes, are seeing sex.

***

The problem isn't
whether a woman
dresses in
liberal or modest ways.

The problem is
men who think
that we exist
for their gaze.

260.

A man looking at a woman posting a nude for her empowerment, not for his gaze-
this is what goes on in his mind through his haze:

Oh, so women have their own thoughts about their bodies and sexual feelings????
They are not just sexualized, designed to be appealing???
They are not just holes to poke???
Women own their own bodies???
I don't get it. Is this a fucking joke???

And then, he wastes no more time
to reach third base-
gets his penis out, whacks his jizz about
marking his territory, all over the place.

***

Men are confused
when women post nudes,
for their self-empowerment
not for the male gaze.

Because men struggle to see
women, outside the dichotomy,
of virgin/whore;
a woman's body-is either/or.

Nudity, to men, is nothing more,
than sex.
Nudity, to women, is so much more,

than sex-
it is an art, a reclamation, a way to express
that "I own my body",
but what men see, in female nudity,
is "sex on a body".
And somehow, someway
the men's vision of female nudity
dominates our everyday.

But
I own this bag of skin,
fuck your interpretation-
I post my nudes, not for dudes
or a male gaze validation.
I post my nudes, for myself
to normalize this body you have sexualized
I post my nudes, for female liberation,
from the narrow view that our bodies
are owned by men, presented to them, for sexual temptation-
this bag of meat, is not yours to eat
feel your fucking starvation.

261.

The reason we don't believe
that a woman in a short dress
or tight skinny jeans
is dressed for herself,
not for male attention,
is because we do not believe, cannot even imagine,
that women
exist outside of the male gaze.

If she is harassed, it is blamed on her choice of dress-
because we cannot even see, the possibility,
that she doesn't exist to impress,
men,
that she is her own person, not an object for sex.

262.

Imagine,
if we begin,
to realize that women,
have sexual desires-
and we police men on what to wear,
tell them it's a sin, if they don't cover their hair.

Just imagine,
that men would feel threatened
from a woman's glare-
that the female gaze would be a thing
and men would worry what women think.

Imagine,
that men won't feel safe or free,
to dress however, or to simply be.

263.

What do
women's clothes
that are worn
in the public space
and in the bedroom,
have in common?

Sexy, is a priority, over comfort.

What do
the public space
and the bedroom,
have in common?

Men.

264.

No, your hijab
does not liberate you
from the male gaze-
it just reinforces,
that you are a sex object
packaged in different ways.

***

If hijab
is something
that God wants
me wear-
then why is
my husband the one
who cannot bear,
to see the wind
dance with my hair?

Who am I wearing it for?

265.

"HIJAB IS MY CHOICE"
she roared at the top of her voice.
Her community began to rejoice,
in celebration of her.

But what about her sister?
The one slut-shamed
for taking her hijab off?
Doesn't her "choice" deserve
the same respect and love?

Hijab is not a choice,
unless you choose to wear one.
Don't look at the woman wearing it,
look at the other one.

How dare you portray hijab as a choice,
when your sister who took it off
has no safe space for her voice?!

***

Women can choose to wear a hijab so easily
and they are celebrated and encouraged.

But what about choosing to take it off?

When that choice does not exist so freely and is not celebrated-
then you never had a choice to begin with.

N.B. In 2018, an Iranian woman, Shaparak Shajarizadeh, was sentenced to prison for taking off her hijab to protest Iran's compulsory hijab law.

266.

Empowerment loves to play dress up.

On some days,
it wears makeup and heels,
mini-skirts and reveals
all sorts of sex appeals.

Other days,
it prefers to be in a loose maxi dress
no makeup, or an attempt to impress.

Some days it wants to show off
other days it couldn't care less.
And sometimes it's in between-
there's no rule on the right way to be seen.

Empowerment wears a different dress
depending on its mood-
but you gotta remember that empowerment isn't about your dress,
it is in your attitude.

267.

Don't judge my oppression
by the scarf hiding my hair
or the short skirt revealing my thighs.

This body I'm in
has been owned by men
dressed up by them,
since the beginning of time.

If you are to judge my oppression
base it on how I dress
my mind-
for that is, what is,
truly mine.

268.

“So how do you suggest we liberate
girls and women?
Strip them off
hijabs,
and put them in mini-skirts?
Strip them off
mini-skirts,
and put them in hijabs?”
they asked with a tone dressed in a style so derogatory.

“No” I replied,
“let them strip
off,
the shelves
of libraries-
and then watch them liberate
from their history”

***

Education is the key, to break us free,
from our shackles
of misogyny.

269.

When we're in front of the mirror
we're programmed to look for our flaws-
we are quick to see cellulite, dark circles under our eyes
or question the symmetry of our nose.

Today
when you look in the mirror
I don't want you to see,
your face, or your body-
I want you to look for
your personality.

Can you see it?

Of course not!

How can you see
the *love*,
in your soul
in the size of your mole?

How can you see
your *kindness*,
in the lines
of your jaw?

How can you see
your *loyalty,*
and *faithfulness*
in the shade of your skin
or your lips?

How can you see
your *integrity*,
in the shape of your breasts
or the width of your hips?

How can you see
your *bravery*,
and *strength*
in the length
of your legs?

That's right- you can't!

So here's a thought
on which I need you to pause-
if you cannot see
all this beauty,
in the mirror
then how can you see your flaws?!

N.B. The images in the mirror are not what they appear to be.

270.

I’m starting to feel
comfortable in my skin,
especially,
where it’s loose and wrinkly.

I’m starting to feel
comfortable in my skin,
and it’s such a strange
feeling
like wearing
your favourite worn out pyjamas
the one that’s washed out
has a few holes
but you still refuse to throw it out
because its familiar comfort,
cannot,
be emulated by anything new.

I’m starting to feel
comfortable in my skin,
I love wearing myself-
it fits so well, to be true.

***

To live comfortably
in your skin,
love yourself
from within.

271.

Tonight
as I lay by your side,
like the shore
sleeping next to the sea,
I want to tell you a story.

I ask your waves
to listen gently,
as they crash into me.

This body,
I carry, carries the ruins of a temple-
the cracks and marks
mark
a history,
of what this body has seen
and everywhere I have been.
This slate isn't blank-
that's why it isn't spotlessly clean.

There has been pain
and there has been joy-
I have been worshipped by some lovers,
and by others,
used as a toy.

But this story I want to tell you
is not about sex-
this body carries more than
a vagina under a dress.

I want you to know,
this body is not a show-
it is a story.

Do you see?

Those rolls rolling around
my stomach
which society calls 'lazy'-
are how I rolled out of
postpartum depression,
when I had my first baby.
Food was my therapy.
What remains on my body
is a sign of my victory.

I'll tell you another story-
this scar sprawled
over my thigh,
reminds me that I didn't die.
It was from when I was a little girl
and dared to hop on
a motorbike
by myself,
I wanted to be like the older boys
not wanting the help
of anybody else,
and I fell
but I got up.
This scar reminds me
that I will never stop.

Do you see?

The cellulite partying around me,
is a celebration
of the day I stopped giving a fuck
about having smooth skin
sculpted
filtered
like a Photoshop.
The world wants my body
to be
a blank slate-
but my limbs aren't up
for this debate.
I have lived
read that again
I have lived!
This body went through life-
stop the shame
stop inducing self-blame
I have lived, I have learned,
I have changed-
how can my body
stay the same?

***

Tonight
as I lay by your side,
like the shore
sleeping next to the sea,
I want you to touch me.

But not like sex
not like everybody else-
I want you to touch my imperfections
without feeling sorry.

Tonight,
touch me in a way that feels like you are reading
each page
of my story.

272.

He's been with
the skinny girl
the fit girl
the curvy girl
and the plus size.

He's been with
the smooth skinned
and the one with cellulite.

He's been with
lots of different shapes and sizes
over the years.

He's been with
every type of woman your eyes can see-
and all of those women he's been with,
are me.

N.B. Our bodies change over time. Our bodies change all the time.

273.

The greatest
love story ever told-
is the one where
you love yourself,
and never withhold.

274.

And in between all the
"I love you's"
and the
"I miss you's"
that I gave away to others-
I forgot to give some
to myself.

***

I've held
so many lovers
with those hands of mine-
but now, it's time,
to hold
myself.

275.

When was the last time
you went out on a date,
with yourself?

When was the last time
you got all dolled up,
for you?
Went out for fresh coffee,
or a slow stew?

When was the last time
you took yourself to the movies
and cried over some silly little scene,
magnified on the big screen?

When was the last time
you took yourself to dance?
Fell in love with yourself
from just a glance?
Who says romance,
has to be between two?
Who says you have to wait
for a man to love you,
for love to come to you?
Look at you!
Not in the mirror, look into your soul
go ahead- realize that you're whole,
and complete.
You don't need to wait for a man
to sweep you off your feet.
Sweep yourself off!

Sweep yourself up,
and fall head over heels
in love with yourself-
you might discover
you don't need anybody else.

Take yourself out on perfect dates,
don't sit there and wait
for the perfect man to come along
to take you to the perfect night-
that's too much of your joy
placed in the hands of a knight.

And anyway- if you don't already love yourself,
and if you don't show him how
you love yourself in the day and at night-
when he finally comes along, how can he compete?
How can he get it right?

***

Perhaps,
the greatest discovery
is self-discovery.

276.

I was 13
when my heart was first broken.
I was a fucking child.
How can your heart break
when you haven't even
fully developed yet?
I was shattered
thinking I will never ever
find love again.

And now as a grown woman
I know why the hurt was deep-
it's because
of those
fucking fairytales I digested-
the girl gets
one chance to fall in love,
one prince
one happily ever after.
That's it.
I was 13, and I fucked it up already.

I lost love
before I even had a chance to understand it.

***

Little girl, fairytales don't tell you this-
you will kiss

lots and lots of frogs
before you find the prince.

277.

There are men
we drown in love with.
And there are men
whose love makes us drown.

278.

"Where are you from?"
he typed

"Why?"
I typed back

The men I meet online
only want to know
the size of my breasts
or how tightly my hips
can hold sex
to stroke themselves
while they type.
This one wants to know where I'm from
he is interested in me, instead of my body
could he be the one?

"Because I want to know if you live close by"
he typed,
"to fuck your flesh instead
of those socks on my thigh".

279.

There is a myth we teach girls
that if you wait long enough,
for the right boy
the first time you have sex,
will be full of joy.

So they wait and wait for prince charming,
but the sex is so bad, it's freakin' alarming.

And they wonder;
what have I done wrong?
Was it too soon? Or did I wait too long?

I'm here to tell you this,
no matter how soon
or how long you wait,
the first time you have sex
won't ever be that great.

Just like learning how to walk,
at first it's slippery, bumpy, lacks rhythm, and you're likely to get a bruise,
but you forget about all that
once you learn how to cruise.

So don't fret,
if it wasn't what you'd expect-
the first time you have sex
is never,
the best time you'll have sex.

280.

If you want
to know
how passionately
a man
would eat you,
give him
half
of a sliced
passion fruit-
without a spoon,
and watch him
troubleshoot.

281.

He boasted to his friends:
"I gave her,
her best night ever!",
and then,
they all laughed together.

So I bluntly said:
"Boy,
you got nothing
on the orgasms,
from my shower head".

***

One of the greatest mysteries of life
is that the tip of the clitoris
has more than 8,000 nerve endings,
and men still cannot find
even one of them.

282.

What is up
with fuckboys
who think that my orgasm
is just an extra side order
that they don't
have to order,
while they're eating sex
at my table?

Fuckboy;
If you don't understand
that my orgasm isn't optional-
you're not sitting down,
on my table for two.
My pleasure is not a side order-
I am the entire menu.

283.

Instead of faking an orgasm
teach him, how to fuck you better-
a man's ego,
is not more important
than your pleasure.

***

If he doesn't know
how to make you come-
don't fake it.
This is exactly how fuckboys
grow egos
the size of Jupiter.

Teach him, or dump him.

But don't ever excuse him
or continue sucking him,
while he sucks
at pleasing you.

Don't live in the hopes that one day,
he will magically realize on his own
how to use his bone-
those things just don't happen.

If he doesn't know, he will never know,
unless you teach him-
the way you taught your dildo.

If you're not in the mood,
to teach him,
or if you tried and he's just no good-
then tell him the truth.
Don't inflate his manhood
by faking it.

Tell him he isn't good
perhaps you'll inspire him to take a class on female anatomy,
(as he probably should).

When you dump him,
tell him the truth
for the sake of the woman after you-
for the sake of the sisterhood!

284.

My first dildo vs. My first boyfriend

	Dildo	**Boyfriend**
Race	Body-safe silicone	Toxic human
Perfect date	Watching a movie in bed	Watching a movie while I give head
Size	12 inch	Size doesn't matter
Best time to have sex	Whenever I am ready	Whenever he is ready
Guidance to find my sweet spots	Needs my help to operate	Needs my help to operate
Sex talk	Listens to me whisper sweet nothings	Listens to himself talk dirty
Orgasm score	Always me	Always him
Relationship duration	Ongoing (pleasure guarantee)	6 months (no warranty)
Overall cost	$30	My sanity and a lifetime of therapy

285.

She was 10,
when she started masturbating.

It felt good, but she didn't know what she was doing.

Pulsating, like the balanced ripples in a game of Ping-Pong.

Her mother,
caught her, and called her, a slut,
and though she didn't know what she was doing-
she understood
that her pleasure is wrong.

And that lesson, stayed with her, for a lifelong.

***

The encouragement
of masturbation,
should be
the first lesson
in sex education-
because it is the way
your body learns,
how it prefers,
to experience
pleasurable sensations.

N.B. Masturbation won't make you blind, or damage your genitals, or use up all your orgasms. (Source: www.plannedparenthood.org).

286.

When I watch porn I see women
with exaggerated hair extensions on their heads
and bald pussies as if puberty never hit,
with makeup that perfectly smudges during the gag of a blowjob
I see women that moan a lot
I don't know whether it's in pleasure or pain
it all sounds miserably the same.

When I watch porn I see women that are obviously pretending to be turned on
fucked without foreplay
coming from penetration alone, all day
like glory holes, called whores
by men with boners that never settle
who all seem to be
portrayed as experts in the female anatomy.

When I watch porn,
I understand the allure of porn for men;
all the women are a projection
of an ancient male fantasy-
sexy,
but non-sexual objects
(their pleasure doesn't matter).
And all the men in porn never face rejection-
clueless,
yet portrayed as sexual experts.

***

Why do we call female sex workers

names
prostitutes, hookers,
sluts, whores,
but we have no names
for the men
who demand their services?

287.

He watches porn intently
gets an erection
feeling elated
oh, so sedated-
without affection
no chance for rejection
or any objection
this is perfection!
He ejaculated.

That is that problem with porn-
it trains men,
to see women,
as pictures.

You do not need to please a picture.

***

The reason why too many women
feel their pleasure is neglected
in copulation,
is because too many men
cannot differentiate
between sex and masturbation.

288.

"Wait, I'm still a bit dry" I said,
as he painfully penetrated
his penile head,
into my shrivelling vagina.

"Let me put on some more lube"
he excitedly reached out
to grab the tube.

"Stop!" I said,
as I firmly paralysed his hand-
"I'm dry, means I need more foreplay, not more lube-
what the fuck is so hard to understand?"

289.

"I think it's sexy
if you swallow", he said,
while his sperm
was still swimming
in the hole in my head.

He said it,
just as I was about to spit-
and it bothers me,
that he,
didn't even ask, if *I wanted* to do it.

I think that he just expected me,
suddenly,
to want to swallow now
just because
he said
it was *sexy*.

***

What is it about men
wanting to enter,
and leave their mark, to conquer,
every hole, every pore
of my body?

290.

When he says:
"I trust you, but I don't trust the guys around you".

What he means:
"I own you, but I don't own the guys around you".

He thinks he owns you,
so he has a right to tell you
where to go or what to do-
sugar-coating his possessiveness and control
by making it seem like he's merely protecting you.

***

Jealousy is not love.
Controlling is not love.
Overprotection is not love.
Suspiciousness is not love.
Possessiveness is not love.
Clinginess is not love.
Demanding is not love.

Maybe we have talked enough,
about what love is-
and we think we already know a lot.

But we will never understand what love is,
if we don't know what it is not.

291.

Do not teach your sons
to protect their sisters
from men who physically abuse them.

Teach your sons
not to
physically abuse women.

Your daughter's protector
could be another woman's oppressor.

292.

"He's a good man
we see him at the mosque
praying five times a day",
they said.

You saw him
in the house of God
as a guest-
guests take off their shoes at the door
wipe off their foot stains
before entering your space
seating their bodies within boundaries you set.
You saw him as a guest
and guests are always polite.
But you didn't see him
in his own house
when the darkness rapes the light.
You didn't see him
beat his wife,
and you did not hear the verbal abuse.
God would weep if he knew,
that this same tongue that chants prayers
is used
to terrorize
somebody,
that those same hands raised in worship
are used
to bruise
a woman's body.

If you want to judge

whether he's a good man or not
don't look at the footprints
that dug a grave on his prayer mat-
instead, look at the fingerprints on the flesh
of the woman he's with;
does he leave marks of love?
A woman's body can always tell you
whether a man is good enough.

293.

The Little Mermaid,
gave up her voice
for a vagina and legs.
This is how we teach girls
that their voices
don't matter during sex.

294.

“Do you consent?”
he asked,
“I don’t know”
I replied.
He got on top of me,
began to ride.
After all, I didn’t say ‘no’.

“Do you consent?”
he asked,
“Maybe”
I replied.
He slid his tongue deep
held my legs wide.
After all, I didn’t say ‘no’.

“Do you consent?”
he asked,
“I think so”
I replied.
He opened my mouth
and came inside.
After all, I didn’t say ‘no’.

“Do you consent?”
he asked,
I shrugged my shoulder,
in reply.
He undid his fly.
After all, I didn’t say ‘no’.

"Do you consent?"
he asked,
I froze in place,
I didn't say 'no'
but I didn't say 'yes'.
He went ahead anyway
and unbuttoned my dress.

In all situations, I felt distress.

If I wasn't consenting, then I was raped
there is no such thing as non-consensual sex.

***

There are so many ways that a woman says 'no'
without literally saying the actual word 'no'
simply because she doesn't know
how to blurt out a 'no'
when a man is running the show.
Women are raised to go with the flow
sit in the background, like a shadow
so they forgo
the ability to form the phonetic sound of 'no',
even when their entire body is clearly saying 'no'.
Men use this an excuse
to act confused
when it comes to consent
"she didn't say no, I don't know what she meant".

But you know what

you fucking twat
let me give you
a clue,
that is clear-cut;
if she didn't explicitly say 'yes',
then don't undress.
If she didn't explicitly say 'yes',
then take it as a 'no'
let it go
keep your dick, tucked below
because while there are so many ways to say 'no'
without saying 'no'-
there is just one way to say 'yes'.
A 'yes' is loud and clear,
there is no pressure or fear
I assure you, with a 'yes'
your gut won't second-guess.

So if you didn't get a clear 'yes'
then don't push her to bed
you fucking dickhead.
'No means no' - simple English, easy
not saying 'yes', also means 'no',
don't be so fucking sleazy.
Consent isn't an option to forgo,
because while a man may see it as a harmless moment of fun
for a woman,
it can fuck her up long after he's done
long after he's gone,
making her lose trust in everyone.
So listen to her, don't just carry on
before you take out your penis
if it's not a clear 'yes'

then it's a clear 'no'.
Your erection, isn't a medical condition-
Let. It. Fucking. Go.

***

"Do you consent?"
he asked,
"No"
I replied.
"But you liked it yesterday"
He went ahead anyway.

"Do you consent?"
he asked,
"No"
I replied.
"But I love you,
I promise I won't hurt you"

"Do you consent?"
he asked,
"No"
I replied.
"But it has been a while,
don't be so fragile"

And you wonder why
women find it hard to say 'no'?
It's because men are taught
to get what they want,
even when a woman

is clearly distraught.
To them,
consent is a game
a woman is an aim
there to claim
just a body to fuck.
They're all the same
the patriarchy is to blame
for this lack of shame.

***

It's not that "not all men" rape
that matters.

It's that "all women" live with the fear
of getting raped.

295.

The most important thing
us women
need to know-
is that at any given moment
we have the *right*
to say 'NO'.

And 'NO' is a complete sentence-
they don't need to ask you 'why?'

And 'NO' is enough-
you don't have to justify.

***

Consent, isn't just about sex.

Consent, is an instinct,
we develop before we have sex.

When your mother *forced* you into that party dress,
that you didn't like.
When your father *forced* you to hug that uncle,
that you didn't like.
When your parents *forced* you to share with that neighbour,
that you didn't like.

You were practicing your natural instinct to consent,
and they were taking it away from you.
So when you get older, and the boys come around for sex,
you force yourself, to say 'yes', to impress
while you feel 'no'- because you don't know,
what else you could do.

***

Even if you
did not verbally say 'no'
it is still
sexual assault.

Even if you
did not verbally say 'no'
it is still
never your fault.

Sometimes
we don't say 'no'
with our tongues-
it doesn't mean
that the men who hurt us
aren't in the wrong.

Sometimes
we don't say 'no'
with our tongues-
sometimes we say 'no'
with our bodies.

Consent is not

only about
what you verbally say-
it is about your body language
and the energy you convey.

If he looks for consent
through his ears alone,
and ignores what his eyes can see-
then he is a rapist
playing the role
of naivety.

296.

The fact that my heartbeats
begin to race
when I'm walking
alone at night,
while a group of men
are just walking within my sight-
shows how my mere existence
brings me so much fright.

***

Nothing is scarier
than the feeling
of not feeling
safe
inside
your own skin.

297.

I crossed the road
despite the red pedestrian light,
because I was being followed
by a group of men, late at night.
And I realized that's how
women live.
Continually assessing
and choosing
one danger over another.

298.

Every woman,
has a map
that maps out
her safe spaces-
stored in the GPS
of her brain.

We register
the grocery stores, the cafes, the bars
where we won't be catcalled
or slut-shamed.

We memorize
the safest route to get there
and what to avoid, and what to wear.

If we're going
somewhere new,
we first go through,
a list of additional ways to feel safe
a survival instinct way to behave;
like having a friend on speed dial
avoid eye contact, keep a low profile
be wary of that cute guy following us,
because things can escalate to hostile
if we simply refuse to reciprocate or smile.

If you think this is ridiculously insane-
what would you think, if I told you, this is just a sample trial?
This is just a tiny glimpse
into a woman's daily lifestyle.

299.

The tram in Dubai
is divided into two sections-
a sign saying 'for men'
and the other 'for women and children'.
Is this meant to be for our protection?
Emphasizing that the only way
for women to be safe,
is to continue to exist in an isolated space?

I can hear that sign
silently saying;
if you step into the area of men,
you can't blame them
if you get assaulted or raped,
you were supposed to be on the other side
if you violate the rule, it's a free ticket for men to ride,
inside,
your body.

To further add to double standards,
if a woman sits in the men's section,
with her husband or father
it's fine-
but men would get a fine,
if they sit in the women's line
(even if with their sister or wife).
What are we saying to women? You need a man to exist safely in the 'male space'?
Otherwise there is no safe place,
for you,

unless we isolate your body and your face,
from men?

Instead of strategies rooted in victim blame,
instead of isolating women with shame,
instead of niqabs, hijabs,
abayas, burqas,
and other forms of public gender segregation-
why can't we make the world a safer place for women, through awareness and male education?

N.B. If only it was that simple.

300.

Sometimes, when articles or TV shows
want to address rape,
they put a trigger warning, in the beginning,
noting that the content might trigger painful memories
for rape victims and survivors.

In my life,
everything
is a trigger
and nothing
comes with a warning.

When a gorgeous guy flirts with me,
I am triggered.

Baby announcements trigger me,
because you need to have had some sort of penetrative procedure
to have a baby.

Lingerie stores trigger me,
because they remind me of sex.

Sex jokes trigger me.
Rape jokes trigger me. You know what else?

When I book an appointment to see my gynecologist,
I cannot sleep for days dreading
the meeting
and praying
that she won't need to do an invasive pelvic exam, or take a vaginal swab.

This has become my life, and I don't know when it will stop.

Everything
triggers me,
and nothing
comes with a warning.

N.B. Approximately 70% of rape victims experience moderate to severe distress- a larger percentage than for any other violent crime. (Source: Rape, Abuse & Incest National Network- www.rainn.org).

301.

"What's your evidence?"
the policeman asked.

This pain I carry,
I wish I can yank it off me
and physically give it to him
as evidence.
But I cannot locate, its exact place
of residence-
is it in my heart or on my body?
Or it is in the remnants
of me, that I lost,
stuck on my assaulter's body?

So now they have to spread my legs
scrape off,
whatever is left
of,
my dignity,
to use as evidence.

While they gather this evidence of my pain,
I must not resist or feel shame
or else they'll accuse me of playing a game-
because we women just do this for fun
accusing men of things they haven't done,
right?

"Why didn't you fight?"
was the next question.

How can I show him
that I did fight
by making myself freeze?
Freeze my body,
to
freeze the moment
to
freeze the pain,
but somehow the hurt still kept going on.
How can I explain?

"Why did you wait that long, to complain?"
he continued.

How can I tell him
that I genuinely thought
I would be okay?
That I thought it was just
a one time bad thing
that happened, on one bad day?
But then it started haunting me,
I relive it on my flesh-
I was raped one time, but it feels like I'm getting raped every day.
How can I tell him, my rapist isn't here anymore, yet his grip isn't going away?

"What were you wearing on that day?"
he questioned.

I was wearing

my trust
on my sleeve,
I was wearing
the faith and the belief
of the good in humanity
like a superhero cape-
How can I tell him that I didn't realize
what I was wearing
can ignite rape?

"What's that mark on your nape?"
he queried.

Is he suggesting
that because I have been
bitten by lovers,
that it's okay for others,
to take a bite too?
How can I tell him
that I do have sex-
but *rape is not sex*
and I'm here to report rape.
I'm not here to report the lovers on my nape.

"We'll call you when we have a conclusion"
he slams the file on his desk.

I walk out, and shut the door
my wound opens up, again,
freshly sore
as I wonder;

How many more times
will I relive this ordeal?
Will my assaulter's punishment last as long as the time
it will take me to heal?

302.

Why is it
that we eagerly believe
a man who says “I did not rape”,
yet we question
a woman who says “I got raped”?

***

You accuse me of being a liar
because I cannot remember the exact details
the exact time, the exact alleyway, the exact location
where I dug my nails
into his body, to defend my body.

You accuse me,
but after the rape,
my memory became hazy,
perhaps as a defence mechanism
to wipe out
the attack
from my head.

I cannot remember the exact story,
but my neurons,
oh, my neurons-
they will never forget.

303.

Let me tell you this;
I was raped before I knew
what the word 'rape' is,
so I did not kick or scream or push away-
I was raped behind the park
in the middle of a sunny Sunday.

Let me tell you this;
I wasn't wearing a revealing dress
I wasn't even wearing breasts
or hips or a butt,
I was raped in the body of a child
so tell me, who is at fault?

I wasn't drunk.
I wasn't out late.
I wasn't even on a date.
I wasn't asking for it
I wasn't asking for anything else-
I was raped and I didn't even know
that I was raped
I didn't have any self-defence.

Let me tell you this;
if you blame victims
for getting raped,
then you think like a rapist.

304.

I was a child.

I was a child in my body
but a woman inside
my underwear.
It takes blood to turn a girl into a woman.
It takes blood to give life.
It takes blood to kill it.

This is how I was raped.
A moment. A flash. A second.
It doesn't take long to rape.
But it stays in your body for a lifetime.

A lifetime.

A lifetime of battles, and therapy, and why me?

Why me?

I could have been so happy right now
I could have been able to trust and love and have sex
without triggers of pain
that tore the flesh of my childhood
carried into my adulthood,
as a souvenir
to remind me
that some men don't need a full moon
to turn from human to werewolf.

***

I was raped in bare daylight.

His hot rage
burned into me
as my bare cold toes,
dug holes,
into sunflower fields.

I was raped in bare daylight.

While children were running around
laughing,
pushing one another in a meadow,
I didn't know where to go,
as my innocence was being
pulled out of me.

I was raped in bare daylight
as my bare cold toes,
dug holes,
to rape the soils below me.
The soils that buried my innocence,
while it was pumping life in me.

I was raped in bare daylight
where God was a witness to see-
now you tell me to hush,
because no one else would believe me
you tell me what happened was a shame

that I will end up taking the blame,
that I should bury this secret
with me when I die.

But it's not a secret. I was raped in bare daylight,
he wasn't ashamed
so why should I?

305.

"Look at the rape statistics in the West", he said
"they are far worse than us.
You know why we are better?
Because our women cover
their bodies
their women don't cover
their bodies.
Look what happens to the nations where women don't embrace modesty!
Look what happens to them-
when women date men
when women go to bars, and have sex, and smoke, and get drunk, and do drugs, and have abortions, and wear mini-skirts!
Look what happens- they get raped!
It doesn't happen to us though,
research the statistics and you'll know
our women don't get raped as often.
Why?
Because they cover their bodies".

"Do you know how statistics are collected?" I asked him,
"our women cover
their bodies
in shame and victim blame,
they don't report their rape.
They don't report their rapist
because then
they will be forced
to marry him-
he broke into her home, might as well make it his own.
They don't report because they will be accused of having had sex

outside of marriage.
They don't report because we don't have laws against domestic abuse
a husband has a right to scream at you, hit you, force himself in you-
you live in his home, might as well make you his own".

Our rape statistics are not better
because our women cover
their bodies.
Our rape statistics are better
because our women cover
their voices.

We don't report our rape.
We don't report our rapists.

N.B. Are our rape statistics better?

306.

We have been conditioned
to think of a rapist
as some monster-shaped human
that hides in the day
and pounces on us at night.

That's why,
when your rapist
turns out to be the boy next door,
or the family man,
or the church goer-
you feel more shock, than fright.

We have been conditioned
to talk about rape
as if it only happens
in some alleyway past midnight,
by strangers who attack the women
that are out alone
drunk and dressed in dresses
with a length that isn't right.

It's time to educate the masses.

Rape penetrates homes
with the sweet scent of apple pie,
by lovers and husbands we once trusted
to leave love
between our thighs.

Rape rips off all styles of clothes
from a woman's body.

Rape happens to girls and to boys, and to practically anybody.

Rape happens at night and during the day,
and at workplaces and schools
and the temples where we pray.

Rape happens to people who speak out loud,
and to those who have no say.

Rape is about control-
it is not about women or sex.
Rape belongs to no time, place,
religion, race,
or dress.
Rape belongs only to the monsters that do it-
nothing, and no one else.

307.

I was raped.

I was raped
and you cannot blame it
on a short dress,
because I wasn't wearing a short dress
nevertheless,
I was raped.

I was raped
and you cannot blame it
on a time of day or a lipstick shade
because I wasn't wearing a lipstick
and I wasn't out late,
but I was raped.

I was raped
and you cannot blame it
on a headphone,
because I wasn't wearing headphones
but I was raped.

I wasn't in a lover's home,
or walking in a dark alleyway
I wasn't drunk or at a party-
what more do you want me to say?

I was raped!

I was raped

and you cannot blame it
on me being a woman,
because I wasn't even a woman
when I was raped.

I was raped
while I was a man,
and I don't fit into your
victim blaming plan
because you never thought that men can,
get raped.

But I was raped.

I was a man
when I was raped,
and I say I *was* a man, because you say men don't get raped
so I say I *was* a man,
because now that I got raped...
Now, I don't know,
who I am.

***

Perhaps you do not have the power, to end rape.

But you have the power, to listen.

When you listen, you end the narrative of shame and self-blame, for victims and survivors.

N.B. 1 out of every 10 rape victims is male. (Source: Rape, Abuse & Incest National Network- www.rainn.org).

308.

"Men get raped too!"
he screamed,
interrupting the female survivor
speaking about her rape-
robbing her from her voice
like the rapist who robbed her choice,
he doesn't understand what's at stake.

"Yes I know, men get raped too"
she gently said,
"come stand by me, instead,
of shouting at me-
it's not my fault, can't you see?
My brother, we are fighting together,
we have the same enemy".

309.

Yes, it is all men.

Not because all men *will* hurt women.
But because all men *can* hurt women.

***

"He was drunk"-
are the words we use
to explain and excuse,
the bad things he does.

"She was drunk"-
are the words we justify
as the reason why,
the bad things happen to her.

310.

When I found out
that Little Red Riding Hood
wasn't eaten by the wolf-
she was actually raped
I realized,
that her story was shaped,
the way it was framed,
was that she was being blamed
for going out alone, talking to strangers-
like she deserved that fate.

That is how we teach little girls to grow into women
who blame themselves, for the actions of the men towards them.

311.

I'm not asking for it.

I'm not asking for it
in my lingerie or baggy jeans.

I'm not asking for it,
even if *you think* I'm being a tease.

I'm not asking for it.

I'm not asking for it
in my mini-skirt or hijab
or in whatever, other,
garb.

I'm not asking for it.

I'm not asking for it
while I'm drunk as a skunk
or while I'm dancing alone at the club
with no one but my favourite song.

I'm not asking for it, all along.

I'm not asking for it.

What is it with men,
when I verbally scream 'NO' they do not hear it-
but suddenly,
they are all are experts with a power bestowed
in reading me,

to decode
body language and dress codes?

I'm not asking for it, until I ask for it.

I'm not asking for it- do you think that I can't ask for it when I want it?
Do you think I'm a passive object?

Fuckboy,
you'd better believe-
that when I want it, I will ask for it and I will ask you too,
if you want to receive.

312.

Do you realize
that men think
they are paying us
for sex?

Whether through
a flower bouquet
or a dinner date,
a diamond solitaire
or a white picket gate-
they expect sex in return
and they make you feel bad if you turn
them down.

Do you realize
that you aren't obligated
to sell sex?
Not for roses
not for love
not for a house-
Do you realize
you aren't obligated to sell sex
even to your martial spouse?

Do you realize
that you don't have to play that game,
where men pay you upfront
and then expect to claim
your body?

You aren't selling sex

so don't let men guilt you
into giving it to them
just because they already paid.
They chose to spend their money-
but you didn't post an ad
saying 'with gifts, you'll get laid'.

313.

The women
he played,
now play
a harrowing tune
in every instrument
he touches...
His piano.
His guitar.
His saxophone.
His penis.

The women you break
will leave you broken, too.
Because you were once
bonded in wounds of womb-
you were once a woman, too.

314.

You told me
"I love you",
but you just loved
my body.

You loved
the silk of my flesh
and
how we would mesh
under the sheets,
how we would hold hands,
on the streets-
like a jigsaw puzzle
for people to see,
how perfectly,
we fit.

You told me
"I love you",
but you just loved
the sound of my loin
when it would moan
your name
burning a hole, through my soul
to fill me,
with empty,
kisses,
and unfulfilled promises-
you loved the idea of me
thinking that you love me
so that I'd give you all of me.

You told me
“I love you”,
but you just loved
my body-
don’t get me wrong, there’s nothing wrong,
with just loving my body,
but you said that you loved ‘me’...
and I am not
just
a
body...

315.

He built a bridge
out of my body
to the land of 'forget';
to forget his pain,
to forget his misery,
to forget his sorrow,
to forget his history.

He built a bridge
out of my body
to the land of 'forget',
and when he crossed over
to the place of 'happiness that's true'-
he burnt the bridge,
and forgot me, too.

316.

I'm done being in a relationship
with your shadow-
you have no time for me
so why do you want to be,
in a relationship?

I'm done having sex with you
while you close your eyes-
while I can see you fantasize
about others.
If you want them,
why do you still fuck me, then?

I'm done being your side dish-
do you know how many others wish,
to taste my love?
You leave me like leftovers, when you've eaten enough
of my meat-
you toss away my bone, you begin to moan
that you want dessert, you need something sweet.

I'm done.
Standing, while you're sitting,
on a table for one.

I'm done.

A relationship is meant to be
reciprocation,
between two.
But in our relationship

we both
only love,
you.

***

And when you say you're done
they begin to threaten.

Why is it called 'revenge porn'?
What is the revenge on?
That I once showed you myself
in a way that nobody else
would see?
And your revenge is because we argued over something else
so now you want to expose my
vulnerability?

The only thing you prove with revenge porn
is that you're an asshole that can't be trusted-
it's the surest way, to keep potential dates away
and everyone you love, disgusted.

N.B. Revenge porn is a criminal offence in some countries around the world.

317.

He hates her
because he loves her
more than he ever loved himself.

318.

“You’re not marriage material”, he said
after he pulled out
from inside her groin
after he penetrated her soul
he must have gone in just to check
what kind of material she’s made of.

What kind of material
must your flesh be moulded of
if you have sex
with every woman you see,
but then when you’ve had enough fun-
you want to settle down
with a woman
that was never touched, by anyone?

***

When you tell me
that a future husband
wouldn’t want me,
if I’ve had previous lovers-
have you considered
that perhaps I don’t want to marry a man
who thinks that a woman exploring her pleasure,
makes her a less than?

319.

Slow down,
where are you going?
Let's bask
in this bed
of dawn roses.
Let's mourn
the midnight, this morning.

You rush to make coffee
to put on your suit,
the one that would suit
the skyscraper office of yours
hanging from the clouds.

I hang onto the threads
of tangled
Egyptian cotton sheets
the miles of Nile,
I lay in them, for a while
against my flesh
like you did, last night
when you won't slow down for awhile.

You want me
when it's dark,
when no one else can see
except the stars and the moon and that one
hundred year old palm tree.
You want me,
but just in a dream, a fantasy.

When the dawn
begins to bite into your bitter skin,
you suddenly say what we did was sin.
When the dawn
wakes up,
breaking down, breaking up
with the rays,
you get up,
into your old ways, too...
to wash me off your cells
because you don't believe
that dreams can come true.

What is it about the dawn
that reminds you of our sin?
I screamed "Oh God!" "Oh God!"
a thousand times last night
yet you didn't think of God...
you kept your fucking penis in,
penetrating my flesh
worshipping my skin
but when the dawn is up, and your dick is down,
you frown
you tell me it was all a big mistake, a sin?!

You rush to make coffee
to put on your suit,
the one that would suit
the skyscraper office of yours
hanging from the clouds.
You think you're closer to heaven
closer to God now?

I am not a pit stop to sit your sin
I am not a pit stop to spit your semen
I am not going to be the woman wrapped, in the promises of your demon.

Slow down,
today you're not going.
Let's bask
in this bed
of dawn roses.
Let's mourn
the midnight, this morning.

Let's mourn, this morning
and that sunburn from hell-
your skin sins so well,
your face is fucking glowing!

320.

We consider her ‘dirty’ when she’s had too much dick
and ‘pure’ when she’s careful with her pick.
But let me ask you this;
If a penis
has the power to make a woman dirty,
why do we call her names,
give her the blame
the shame
and dub her as filthy-
isn’t it the penis that should be guilty?

***

“What’s your problem?” he asked
when I confronted his hypocrisy
his penis has entered
dozens and dozens of women’s bodies
and now he calls them ‘dirty’
now he wants his mother to find him
a new virgin hole where no man has been
because she would be clean
enough,
to make a wife out of.

“What’s your problem?” he asked

My problem is that you don’t see
that your penis is the one that is dirty
according to your logic, those women were clean
before you,
before you

penetrated their bodies with your ego
rendering them "damaged goods"
it was YOU
that damaged them.
My problem is that you don't see
how your misogyny
damages us all-
you, them, and me.

321.

Dear Future Husband,

I am confused.

If sex
is the most sinful taboo,
and the worst thing
I could possibly do-
then why I must I save my virginity
to give it
to you?

***

My virginity, is mine.
It is not a giveaway
for a man, on our wedding day.

***

Virginity
is not something
that when you give,
it's forever gone.

It feels different,
after each lover-
not just your first one.

322.

I walked into the grocery store
wearing a white wedding dress-
people astonishingly said;
“you’re here to buy stuff,
there’s no need to declare
you’re a virgin in bed”.

I walked into school
wearing a white wedding dress-
people astonishingly said;
“you’re here to study,
there’s no need to declare
you’re a virgin in bed”.

I walked into work
wearing a white wedding dress-
people astonishingly said;
“you’re here to work,
there’s no need to declare
you’re a virgin in bed”.

I walked into my wedding
not wearing a white wedding dress-
people astonishingly said;
“you must wear white,
to symbolise
your virginity hasn’t bled!”

“No” I said
“I won’t wear a white dress.
I’m here for a union of sharing and caring,

not to be used as sex-
there's no need to declare
whether or not
I'm a virgin in bed".

***

If the hymen could speak
it will tell you about
all the women it held
as prisoners
behind fragile skin,
a bondage in, centuries of oppression.

If the hymen could speak
it will tell you about
all the women it kept
captive
as the warden of sin,
burying their desires within.

If the hymen could speak
it will tell you about
all the women it killed
in the name of honour
in the humiliation of virginity checks-
and how it kept all women in check.

If the hymen could speak
it will tell you that it cannot speak,
because it has no tongue-
and it has no other purpose or function

except to make women feel
that their pleasure is wrong.

***

If only,
we value
not breaking
a woman's heart
the way we value
not breaking
her hymen.

N.B. The United Nations agencies and the World Health Organization (WHO) call for a ban on virginity testing (performed by inspecting the hymen for tears and/or inserting two fingers into the vagina). This procedure is medically unnecessary, painful, and a discrimination against the human rights of girls and women. Additionally, there is no scientific evidence that virginity testing can actually prove whether vaginal intercourse had occurred.

323.

Twenty years later,
I still think about
the boy next door
and the many more
boys I rejected,
all because I was trained
that boys can't be trusted-
that they just want me for sex,
and when they're done with me
nobody else,
who's half decent, would want me.

But what about me?
What about what I want?
What about satisfying my desires,
when I feel turned on?
What about enjoying the pleasures
that my body was born,
with?
What about the idea that sex is for ME,
that it's not something I give?

Twenty years later,
I still think about
the boy next door
and the many more
sexual experiences I denied myself-
all because I was trained
that sex belonged to my future husband,
that MY body belonged to somebody else.

324.

I don't know
what it feels like
to be touched by hands
that did not take my hand
in marriage.

I wonder,
how would other men
trail their fingers
to trace
my landscape,
without colonizing me?

I wonder,
how would it feel
if I was kissed
a thousand different times
by a thousand different knights
on a thousand different nights?

I wonder,
how would I orgasm
from a momentary pleasure
a one night stand,
a no romance,
a not leading to, asking for my hand,
a not even holding hands?

For all my life,
I've only ever been, with one man.
And I love him, oh so dearly dear...

but I just wonder,
with other men, how would sex
feel?

325.

Why I saved my virginity for marriage:

- Because I was scared of revenge porn,
ending up all over the internet
and in my dad's office screen at home.

- Because I was scared of trusting lovers who turn out to be fuckboys
history repeats itself,
and I know women are used like toys.

- Because I was scared of getting pregnant and causing my family shame,
to bring to the world a child
that has no father to claim.

- Because I was scared that if I lost my virginity,
no man would ever want to marry me,
and I would end up lonely.

It took me years to see,
I saved myself, because I was scared of everybody else-
not because I believed in virginity.

326.

One day,
she couldn't control
herself anymore,
this sweet prince charming
swept her off the floor,
right as she fell, into hell,
madly in love,
words weren't enough-
she wanted more.
She wanted to press her skin
on the abs knitted all the way across his chest,
she wanted his fire
to blow up her dress-
she had sex.
(*They* had sex).

They killed her
for having sex,
because a woman's fragile hymen,
is not supposed to break
as it carries the weight
of entire centuries
of oppression, suppression, tradition....

They killed her
for having sex,
because sex is a deadly sin.
But to have sex you need at least two people,
so why didn't they also,
kill him?

N.B. As many as 5,000 women are murdered each year in the name of honour killings, many of them for the "dishonour" of having been raped. (Source: United Nations Population Fund).

327.

If I have to die
for a man's honour-
I will proudly live
with no honour.

***

Women are not bags
to store your honour,
or limbs, for you, to pluck.

Women, just like men,
are born free;
to live, to be,
and to choose who to fuck.

328.

I will touch myself
without your consent.

This body is mine.
I have spent
years and fears
and thousands of times
convinced it was yours-
to set the rules
that rule
the contour
of my skin,
and all that lies within.
Your lies trained my limbs-
anything other than your touch,
is sin.

But this body is mine
and if you won't give it back-
I will forcefully take it.

I will touch myself
without your consent
in places you never even spent
a second, to try to understand.
Places where
you placed your hand
to leave your pain
and whiskey stains
like jumping out of a moving train.

My body is not an asylum for the insane.

I am not a pit stop for your sins
to cleanse yourself,
leaving rotting limbs.

It will take time
to take back what's mine
to understand that I don't need your permission.

I start today.

I will touch myself
without your consent.

***

We teach our daughters
not to have sex,
when we should be teaching them
not to have bad sex.

329.

When I fight virginity culture,
I am not fighting against the woman
who *chooses* to be a virgin-
I am fighting against a system that wants to *control* a woman's body.

When I fight sex culture,
I am not fighting against the woman
who *chooses* to have sex-
I am fighting against a system that wants to *control* a woman's body.

330.

Sometimes
women just want to play,
we don't look for prince charming every day.

Sometimes
we just want a cheap toy,
to fuck around
with a fuckboy.

There is this misconception
that women
don't date to play,
that each man is measured for fit
for our wedding day,
that we are on a constant hunt for a happily ever after-
but sometimes, we want things
knowing well they'd end in disaster.

Sometimes
women just want to play, with a cheap toy,
to fuck around
with a fuckboy.

And there is nothing wrong with that-
momentary lust isn't just for men,
take off your judgemental hat.

331.

It is perfectly acceptable,
for women to be sexualized
by men.
But if a woman voluntarily chooses to be sexual,
she is slut shamed by them.

Why?
Simply because if she takes charge
of her sexual expression,
instead of remaining a passive player,
in this male game
they assume that she consents to what men see-
that she is a slut,
for what else can she be?

***

The reason men use the terms
'whore' or 'slut'
as an insult,
towards women-
is because they expect women
to be *ashamed*
for being sexually active
and enjoying their bodies.

***

All my life I was taught
that sex is my only power

as a woman.

Men can rule the world
their voices loud and heard
respected and preferred.
But the only thing I can use
to get a man to hear me,
is the power to seduce
to bring him down to his knees
spread my legs, make him beg please.

I won't apologize for using
my sexual power
to empower,
myself.

Men use and abuse, the privilege of being a male
I won't treat my only patriarchal privilege as taboo and frail.
When I am in control of my body, men entail
that I must back down,
but then they takeover, and my body isn't for sale.

I know all the tricks of blackmail-
so suck it, suckers,
I'll use my sexual powers
to tip the fucking scale.

332.

Little Red Riding Hood
went out for a walk
alone in the woods.
She's a whore!

Cinderella
stayed out dancing
till midnight.
She's a whore!

Snow white
leaves her home
and lives with roommates
(who happen to be men).
She's a whore!

Ariel and Jasmine
wore crop tops
showing off skin.
They are whores!

And then there was me,
a child
enchanted by every story.
Tell me more!
Tell me more!
Oh how I would love
to be a whore!

333.

As an experiment,
cut out my female nipples
and paste a pair
of male nipples on me-
would you still say
I must not set my nipples free?

As an experiment,
cut out my female locks
and give me a man's hair-
would you still say
hijab is a garment, I must wear?

As an experiment,
cut out my female skin
that is so smoothly shaved,
and give me hairy male skin-
can I wear a mini-skirt,
without you saying it's a sin?

As an experiment,
cut out my vulva
give me a penis instead-
would you still judge me
for how many lovers
I fuck in my bed?

As an experiment-
I want you to see
women and men
through the lens of equality.

How much better,
would our world be
as an experiment?

334.

The old man at the corner store
with the conservative views
selling stale news,
that everybody
already
read on Twitter, some hours ago-
looks at me,
like fresh celebrity
gossip.
With his silent grin
I read the subtitles
under his chin;
"I know you had sex"
"You're wearing last night's dress"
"Your makeup is smudged,
and your hair is a mess"

And it's not just him,
the whole neighbourhood is judging me-
for daring to walk out in daylight
dressed in evidence of a sex spree.

So what?
Just because last night I had fun,
today I must bow my head down
and do a 'Walk of Shame'?
A man is high-fived for having casual sex,
with women that
he doesn't even know by name.
But it takes two to tango- so who are those nameless women?
If he is celebrated, why are they treated with shame?

We are not
passive objects,
passed around
in a double standard game.

It's time to proudly reclaim.

Let tomorrow's newspaper headlines
boldly exclaim;

There will be a star
carved above the name,
of every woman
proudly stepping
on that fucking
'Walk of Shame'.

335.

When does
cheating begin?

When I started fantasizing
about that other, lover?

Or

When I actually,
slept with him?

336.

He asked me
how many lovers
I have had before him,
and I didn't know
what to tell him.

Who counts as a lover?
The ones who loved me more than I could love them,
or the ones whose love
made me suffer?

***

"Must I tell him my history?"
she asked,
feeling the need
to 'come clean'
about how many men have been
running around her meadow.

"Why do you feel that you must tell him?" I asked her in reply.

"I don't know...I want to be honest" she said, with a sigh.
She clearly doesn't want to tell him,
but feels like she's hiding a lie.

What is this sense of obligation we feel
to tell men,
what we have done before them?

As if our bodies and hearts are products
that we are selling on *eBay*,
so we need to have a description;

Condition: 'used'
Quantity: '[insert number] previous lovers'

Your past doesn't belong to him
you don't owe him
any explanation.
If you want to tell him,
it should be your choice, to share this information.

But you shouldn't feel any sense of obligation
if you don't want to tell him, it is totally okay.
You're not giving him your past (you cannot give him your past),
you're giving him your present, you're giving him today.

337.

I was not made
to be saved,
for one man-
like a file on the computer
sitting in a new folder
waiting to be filled,
with his ideas.
I am not waiting wide open
for a man to come stuff me
with his desires, like a tortilla.

I was not made
to be saved,
for one man.

I did not come
into this body, in this life,
waiting to be chosen
to be one man's wife.
No.

This body, objectified
by millions
is not made to be won,
by one.
I decide what gets to be done
with the moon of my passion
with the heat of my sun.

I was not made
to be saved,

for one man.

I am not the prize in the contest.
I am not a man's conquest.

I was not made
to be saved,
for one man.

This body is mine-
do you understand?
And I want to explore it,
I will not wait for a man
to colonize and conquer my land.

I was not made
to be saved,
for one man, by one man-
I will have them all
fuck the dicks, suck the balls
and eat all the pussy I can.

338.

I kissed her,
the way men used to conquer
the landscape of my flesh.

I touched her,
the way men used to rummage
underneath my dress.

"What are you doing?" she said.

"I'm loving you" I replied.

"But that is how men love women" she cried,
"My love,
let me show you the way
a woman loves".

339.

"How did you,
find out,
you were gay?"
he asked.

Expecting me to tell him a story,
wrapped neatly
around a time and a day.

But instead of answering him,
I asked him,
to narrate;
"How did you,
find out,
you were straight?"

340.

Plot twist:

And the princess
married
a princess-
And the prince
married
a prince-
and they all
lived
fucking happily
ever
after.

The End.

341.

I’ve been touched so slow, the way eternity moves
by lovers who tried
to pause lifetimes
on the pulse of my skins.
I’m out of your league, *Nemo*-
I’ve been kissed by dolphins.

342.

Is it just a coincidence,
that in this life I am expected
to give myself to one God
and
to give myself to one Man?

What is the difference
between each oath?

What is the difference
between God and Man,
if I am expected
to submit to both?

343.

Do you love him,
because you love *him*?
Or because you love
the way he loves you?

Stop. Reflect.
Does this ring true?

Do you love him,
because you love *him*?
Or because you are afraid of
what would happen to you,
if you stopped loving him?

***

Perhaps what I truly miss
is not you-
Perhaps I miss the me that I was
when I was with you.

***

You see, I could be,
embraced by this whole big world,
the whole world wrapped around me,
but I still feel lonely
when I still feel you on my skin, literally touching me outside in,
yet you aren't...
physically, with me.

Perhaps, if I wash your memory
away with this old bottle
of bottled up bourbon,
perhaps I'll forget how you feel
on my body, in my bones,
perhaps when I finally forget you,
perhaps I will no longer
feel alone.

344.

Why are women so afraid of being alone?

We're willing to redecorate, refurnish, refurbish
those bodies that are our homes,
just to keep lovers from straying away.
Grooming, brooming, perfuming- doing whatever it takes to make them stay.

We're so afraid of being alone
with our bodies,
we're willing to house them, rent them, accommodate them, make them homely for somebody
else.

And then, when those lovers stop paying rent,
when all their time is spent
outside this home we built for them,
when they treat us not as a home
but just a hotel bed
to come to for a nap or a quick fuck-
we begin to smash down our homes, instead of those schmucks.
We beat ourselves up
Why didn't I try harder? Why wasn't I enough?!

My love,
you'll know if he's the one
because you won't have to refurbish-
he will love you the way you are.
And you will settle in
a kind of love, where you won't ever feel afraid of being alone-
your body will rest, from the need to impress

and his body,
will feel like home.

***

If he's the right one,
you won't *fall*
in love.

You will *rise*.

345.

And then,
he came along-
not a prince dressed as a frog
not a knight in shining armour
not a saviour riding a white horse
not in any form I was taught to look for.

He came,
just as himself-
and oh, how lovely that was.

***

All my life
I had to choose between
feeling safe
or
falling in love,
until I met you-
and I felt safe
enough,
to fall, deeply,
in love.

346.

I’ve been with jerks,
and I’ve been with fuckboys.

I’ve been with dogs,
and I’ve picked up chew toys.

And I am grateful for all that I have been
because without it I wouldn’t have seen,
that I deserve a king-
not to save me, but to sit next to me
for I am already a queen.

347.

You know what it feels like?

It feels like I'm in
Santorini,
with you,
drinking wine
till half past nine.
Going for walks
and climbing up
tall talks,
the kind
that take me deeper
inside your mind.

It feels like that time I let my hair down
and listened to the sound
of your heart beating
on the edge of your flesh,
while your hands trekked up my dress-
not because you wanted to conquer my skin
but because you genuinely wanted to see
the glow in my eyes, when I'm horny
when I unleash my raw animalistic Goddess
when I unbind my mermaid legs,
to set my sex,
free.

It feels like I'm about to dance,
with the tips of my toes
on the soft whispers,
of your moonlight romance.

That's what it feels like
we're doing-
every time
we simply
just hold hands.

348.

I've adorned this body
with so many charms;
yet it is the most beautiful
when I am naked and free
in the confinement
of your arms.

***

You are
my favourite dress,
every time we have sex,
I don't want to strip
you off me.

349.

Perhaps,
I don't want him
to give me promises
or to be the groom on my wedding day.

Perhaps,
I want him
just to give me hope,
for today.

350.

Bed sheets,
blush
from the way
we make love.

Love,
that penetrates
our souls,
and between the cracks of our walls.

Walls,
cripple then come
closing in,
around me and him.

Him,
is where I want to die
and to bury all my shame.

Shame,
that shudders and shatters with my orgasm-
from his orgasm, I want to be born,
all over again.

351.

Tonight,
I won't strip my clothes
to reveal to you my body.

Tonight,
I will strip my skin and bones
to reveal to you my soul.

***

Tonight,
I want you to fuck
my mind.

Touch me,
but not physically.
Touch me
the way you touch the spines of books.

Take me in,
but not physically.
Take me in,
the way you take in words from books.

Tease me,
but not physically.
Tease me,
the way the greatest storytellers plant hooks,
then fold and fondle my pages-
tonight, it's not about my looks.

Tonight,
I want to know what it feels like
when you love me
inside out.
I want you to go all in,
to know what I'm all about.

Tonight,
don't fuck my body
(so many men just fuck a woman's body)-
tonight, I need something hard inside.

Tonight,
don't fuck my body,
I want you to fuck my mind.

352.

Strip me,
to my naked cells.
Touch me in places,
only God knows too well.

Kiss me,
like the end of time
when there are no more worlds
left to rhyme.

Love me,
like lemon drops
on oceans of troubles
that never stops.

Whisper
that Bossa Nova song
dressed in a time
stolen by the young.

Hold me,
let's dance
on the shadows
of the tiptoes
of the moon
on this jolly June.

Take me,
to your heart
but don't break your chest for me.

For when it's true love, my love
believe it or not, it's that easy.

***

Because
I am truly me
and you are truly you-
this love
is truer than true.

353.

"I need to see your marriage certificate", the hotel receptionist said with a 'I'm just following the rules' stamp on his forehead.

As a local citizen of an Arab country,
you cannot book a hotel room if you aren't married,
and you cannot check-in without your martial spouse.
You cannot rent an apartment, with a partner,
or legally live in a house.

That is the rule
to ensure
locals have no places
to have sex outside of marriage-
no sex outside a marital home
no pressing of your skin, against a lover's bone.
No casual encounters, no one night stands,
no forms of physical pleasure, not even holding hands.

The government owns our sex lives,
it sleeps between our thighs
it regulates our orgasms
and who gets to come inside.

The government owns the borders of our bodies
and our sex organs,
a marriage license is a visa
to grant entry to one person-
to tour under your clothes
to penetrate your pores
and mark their territory upon your flesh.
You only get one person, and only when the government says 'yes!'

No sex before marriage,
you can't even test out just a few fucks,
you commit
to a *Kinder Surprise* situation
sometimes,
a *Jack-in-the-box*!

354.

‘Spinster’
is just a label
to shame a woman
for not settling down
for less than she deserves.

355.

He pulled a daisy from the meadow
and planted her behind my ear.

He pulled her away from her sisters, her mothers,
and everyone she found dear.

He told me, "You look beautiful today"
with the daisy wilting,
to hear what else he was to say.

And that's when I realized the truth
about picket fences,
white dresses,
and sparkly diamond rings-
men express love,
by isolating
then killing
beautiful beings.

356.

We were running around lush fields
tickling the greens with our bare feet.
We were picking out white daises
when they picked out our white dresses,
and when the roses
bloomed red
they said
it's time to wed,
plucked us
locked us
convinced us
this beauty belongs indoors
in beds
in strange homes,
of strange men
who keep saying, again and again
"this beauty of yours, is now mine".
But how can roses continue
to bloom, without sunshine?

***

The price tags read;
$0.99
$10,000
$30,000

Those aren't price tags on chewing gum, or a car, or the apartment I rented.
Those were the price tags,
on the *brides*,

of the last three weddings I attended.

N.B. 'Bride price' is a traditional practice in many cultures, whereby the groom would pay the bride's family an agreed price in return for her hand in marriage. This practice often leads husbands to believe they have a right to do whatever they want with their wives because they "bought" them. Also poor families are eager to "sell" their young daughters in child marriages, as a means to earn money. (Source: www.mifumi.org – an international non-government women's rights organisation based in Uganda).

357.

Can you imagine
living in a world
where falling in love
is forbidden?
Where, from the day
you are born
you're auctioned to marry
your male cousin?

What if,
he isn't my type?
What if,
there's no chemistry?
What if,
I'm revolted, fucking someone
whose blood
runs in me?

What if,
I don't want to marry,
him or any other man?
How can you easily seal
my sexual fate?
What if,
I'm a lesbian?

***

What if, he can't please me?
What if, he has no clue how to touch a woman?
What if, the sex turns out to be awful?

What if, when we make love, I close my eyes to see other men?
What if, when we make love, he closes his eyes to see other men?
What if, the hairs on his back, and the smell of his semen,
sticks onto our bed sheets?
What if, he cheats?
What if, I can't stand, leaving the toilet seat up, or listening to his shit stir then flush?
What if, I never feel that rush
of my heart beats racing after one another?
Oh God! What if, I never love him, Mother?!

N.B. In 2018 a mother from UK, who took her daughter to Pakistan and forced her marry a relative almost twice her age, has been sentenced to four-and-a-half years in prison. (Source: BBC news).

358.

Father-
if you must choose the man I marry,
then you must come over every morning
to prepare his butter and bread.
And at night, when he turns off the light
you must come cover to fuck him, instead
of me.

Father-
if you must choose the man I marry,
my only wish
is for you and him,
to live together happy.

N.B. The United Nations' International Labour Organization (ILO) and the Walk Free Foundation published figures showing that 15 million people over the world were trapped in forced marriages in 2016.

359.

Men with a record
of violence and abuse
must not be allowed
by law to get married,
or reproduce.

In the workplace,
you could be denied a job you apply to
if you have a criminal history-
so why can a man apply and get accepted into marriage,
despite a record stating that he is predatory?

360.

"I don't like having sex"
she confessed
to her gynaecologist.

She blurted the words,
though she wasn't asked-
she needed to tell someone
that she waited all her life
for a husband's touch
and it turned out to be
not so much
not at all
electrifying, exciting...
And now she is dying,
with regret to rewind her life-
fuck virginity, she should have tried him out,
before she became his wife.

He's on the phone
while turned on
while fucking her,
he's talking to his mother
about what he had for dinner!

He's poking at her meat -
grilling, grinding
her flesh under his heat.

Sex is a chore,
even wiping the floor

has more friction, more glistening, more wetness...
She envies the erotic romance between rugs and tiles.

He is naive to the fact that
female flesh can feel
pleasure -
he thinks the folds of her skin,
are there just to skim
on the way
to his orgasm.

He thinks sex is just for him.

***

How many women
are trapped in a marriage to a man,
who doesn't know-
how the female orgasm would ripple,
and then gently flow?

361.

Don't tell me it's wrong
to spread my legs wide,
and tell him what I want inside.

My friends all say
when you get married, don't ever wear a thong
because your husband might wonder
how do you know about sexy lingerie?
"A sexual woman, is not sexy", my grandmother would say.

My 20 year old cousin thinks
that if a man kisses her
she can get pregnant-
and her naivety is prized
by her mother, advertised
in women gatherings
for others to see
how pure her daughter is.

Fuck this narrative of naivety.
Why pretend, when I deserve to be?

I deserve to be,
sexual, not sexualized.

I deserve to be,
prioritized, not prized.

I deserve to feel,
the pulse between my thighs.

I deserve to tell him what I want inside-
I am not an object
made of clay and mud.
I am not a fleshlight
or a blow up sex doll-
I am a woman, and I have desires
and I deserve to feel them all.

362.

The moon strips from her darkness
throws her shadow on top of the sea's tide
together they bounce in a familiar rhythm
making love all night.

I sit on the shore with the stars
watching this erotic pornography.
They invite us all to join in
to marinate our skins,
between shades of shadows and sweet salts of the sea.

So we take the plunge
and jump-
the stars are all over me.
This erotic show in the ocean
has now become an orgy.

When the dawn rises
they all rush away,
and I am left alone again,
simmering in my marriage
to the sorrow sea.
Forgive me God, for I have sinned,
but it was only a fantasy.

363.

They say, with dismay:
Divorce! Look at the high divorce rates!
Look how awful and broken
our world has become!

I say, with a hooray:
Divorce! Look at the high divorce rates!
Look how women are standing up for themselves-
dumping men who are scum!

***

The reason we do not celebrate
breakups and divorce
the way we celebrate getting together and getting married,
is because we are taught
that self-love is selfish-
that loving someone else,
(even if it makes you unhappy)
is more valuable than loving yourself.

It's time to change that.

Let us have ceremonies,
for breakups and divorce-
gather family and friends
to witness self-love,
in all its mighty force.

Let us rejoice,
divorce and breakups-

let us announce our commitment
to always choose self-love.

Let us celebrate,
the high divorce rates-
those statistics only mean
that more people are choosing self-love
instead of staying unhappy,
saying “it’s too late”.

N.B. Every 13 seconds, there is one divorce in America. (Source: Wilkinson & Finkbeiner Family Law Attorneys).

364.

Don't tell me
we don't need feminism anymore,
that women have already
attained equal human rights.

Instead, tell me
do you treat a woman
as a human,
once one of her eggs is fertilized?

***

A fetus
matters more
than the woman carrying it
because that fetus
could be a male,
or at the very least,
another female that could potentially produce another male.

It's not pro-life vs. pro-choice.
It's pro-male vs. pro-choice.

***

If a man is against abortion
he should get
a vasectomy.

After all, it is his sperm

that causes an unwanted pregnancy.

365.

To say that the fetus
is a life,
in a womb-
is to say that the dead
is a life,
in a tomb.

***

If a fetus
is a living
creation,
if abortion
is a killing
accusation-
how many
potential fetuses
have men killed,
in masturbation?

N.B. In 2017, Texas lawmaker Jessica Farrar called for men to be fined for masturbating.

366.

My could-be child.

My could-be child.

I love you so,
but I also know
this womb
isn't ready
for you to grow.
And maybe,
it never will be.
So I'll scream goodbye,
but silently.

My could-be child.

My could-be child.

I know that
only you,
can feel, what I truly feel-
my struggle
inside.

My could-be child.

My could-be child.

I'm saving you

so that you,
won't have to, too,
struggle
outside.

***

Abortion, is not killing.
Abortion, is saving a life,
from a life
that would kill it.

367.

We make women
feel guilty
for getting an abortion.
But what about the women
who feel guilty
for not getting one?

Perhaps you know about the guilt
of walking in the wrong direction
or fucking the wrong lover.

But do you know about the guilt
a woman feels
when she regrets
becoming a mother?

***

Did you want to become a
mother?
Or did you feel like you had no other,
choice?
That to be a woman, you must learn,
how to cook and clean
and turn your body into
a baby-making machine,
for men
to insert sperm
while you create clones
of them?

Did you want to become a
mother?
Or were you socially conditioned
and groomed to aspire,
to be no other?

368.

He was
a bundle of joy,
a rosy peach skinned
baby boy.

Nine months ago,
she was
a new bride,
her husband pinned her to the bed
and spread her legs wide.
She told him it hurts,
he told her to hold on, and then he came inside.
He broke her heart in her chest, and then he robbed her pride.

She grew pregnant with pain-
a swollen belly, from swallowing shame
because her mother told her, she was being insane;
husbands don't rape.

But what's insane is that she doesn't know
her father did this, years ago
and her mother doesn't have the language to know;
husbands do rape.

So here she is
a product of rape,
producing another product of rape.

He was
a bundle of joy,

a rosy peach skinned
baby boy.
He took his father's name,
and his pointy nose, too
and if she doesn't tell him 'no'- he might take rape, too.

***

My baby,
how can I tell you
that the blood
in your veins,
is born from
my pains?

My baby,
how can I tell you
that your limbs
are kicking around,
because mine
were pinned down?

My baby,
how can I tell you
that you're here,
because I couldn't escape?

How can I tell you
my baby,
that you were born out of rape?

369.

While his wife was getting
an episiotomy,
he laughed, and asked the doctor
to tighten up her vagina,
by adding an extra stitch.

The doctor looked at him
with concern and asked:
Why? How small is your dick?

N.B. The ‘husband stitch’ is an extra stitch given after a vaginal birth, often without consent, to supposedly tighten the vagina for increased pleasure of a male sexual partner. There is no medical need for it, and it can result in painful lasting consequences for women. (Source: www.healthline.com).

370.

Seven months postpartum
people ask her
if she's pregnant.
"No"
she would say,
"I just have a belly that won't go,
away"

"It's okay"
I reassured her,
"Fuck what people say-
you are Goddess
for you created a human
in this factory,
that is now a hanging belly,
if anything- it is a powerful reminder
of what your awesome body,
has the stamina to carry!"

***

"Are you pregnant again?" someone asked me,
three years after
I had my first baby.

I wasn't pregnant,
I was just wearing
a different body.
My mom-tum
proudly protruded
above my c-section scar-

I wore more shades on my stretch marks
than a soldier,
bruised from war.

That snide comment
was expected to shame me
for living in a "mom-body"
and
for not bouncing back-
as if my pre-maternal body
is just hanging in my closet, and I'm too lazy,
to simply pull it off the rack.

That snide comment
got me thinking
how women
aren't allowed to take space-
the only excuse,
for my gut to hang out,
is if I was carrying,
another human, in its place.

N.B. Many women do not lose the pounds they gained during pregnancy. (Source: research by Dr. Loraine Endres).

371.

I went to the kiddie pool
with all the other moms,
hiding under cover-ups
that fail to hide our tums.

Sure, I miss my
pre-baby body.
Sure, I feel like I'm wearing somebody else's body.
But would you take a look at this?
It's fucking awesomeness!

I was a blank slate, now I'm a full page-
a canvas of cellulite,
stomach rolls,
and stretch marks too,
carefully painted in a roaring red
and shades of badass blue.

It's men that taught us,
such a body isn't desired,
so now you think that
a cover-up is required.
But would you take a look at this?
It's fucking awesomeness!

Moms, let's celebrate
the amazing marks
that document evidence
of what our bodies can do.
This celebration is not for the men (fuck them),
this is for all the other moms,

this is for me and for you;
if I take off my cover-up,
will you take yours off, too?

372.

I am exhausted.

I cannot find the
language to describe
how much I am struggling
in motherhood,
how much I despise
the routine of motherhood,
yet
at the same time,
I am willing to die
for the love of my son.

I cannot find the
language to describe
this contradiction,
because there isn't one.

***

How many mothers out there,
love their kids to death?

No I mean, literally-
Literally, wake up each morning
with no proper funeral, no period for mourning,
and just bury their sense of self
under the dress
of a 'mother'?

I wonder,
how many mothers out there
have forgotten where they left their peace of mind,
but remember the exact places to find,
where their child's
favourite toys tend to hide?

I wonder,
how many mothers out there
have forgotten how to sit down and have a proper meal,
but remember exactly how their child would feel
if their plate of food sat next to the plate of peas?

I wonder,
how many mothers out there
have forgotten to treat themselves to that overdue me-time,
to go to the movies, or the spa,
or buy a new bra,
but remember to take their kids out to play,
every single day?

I wonder,
how many mothers out there
look at pictures
of perfectly happy moms on Instagram,
and wonder: is this real?
If so, then why do I always feel...
tired?
Happy, but tired
loving, but tired
giving, but tired
tired, but tired.

Such strange contradictions
that I cannot explain,
am I even allowed to complain
without being seen
as....a monster?

Because what kind of mother
would say she's tired from being a mother?
From stripping her needs
to put on the dress,
of everyone else
coming first?
Aren't all mothers supposed to love doing this?
Isn't having kids a blessing,
isn't motherhood a bliss?

How many mothers out there
live like this?
Born each morning, to die each day,
for the love of their kids?

They don't see your pictures on Instagram,
but it doesn't mean you don't exist.

I'm here to tell you this,
when you try to find
a place to hide
to cry
between the walls of your home-
I can hear you Fellow Mother
and you are not alone.

373.

Perhaps one doesn't need
a degree in rocket science
or to graduate from an Ivy League school
to do what I do,
but I wonder, what would this world look like
without this highly demanding, unpaid job
that mothers lovingly do?

***

The worst thing that ever happened
to the family unit
is not mothers who left the house for a career-
it is fathers who do not realize
that their role in the household, is not to kick back with a beer.

The worst thing that ever happened
to the family unit
is not mothers who left the house for a career-
is fathers who do not realize
that childcare and housework is also their responsibility too,
that they must do
their share,
so that mothers aren't stretched into despair,
working two full time jobs, at home and outside,
wondering how they can "have it all", without the stress that wrestles inside.

The worst thing that ever happened
to the family unit
is assuming that the home is a woman-only job.

No, the problem isn't that both parents are working outside the home- the problem is entitlement and men who are slobs.

N.B. A U.S. survey shows that 75% of mothers with partners say they do most of the parenting and household duties. One in five mothers says not having enough help from their partner is a major source of daily stress. (Source: www.today.com).

374.

I wanted to go on holiday with my toddler son
but then I realized I would have to actually travel,
get a real plane ticket and board a real plane,
when just taking a trip
to the toilet with my son
is enough to drive me insane.

I wanted to go on holiday with my toddler son
but then I realized I would have to actually pack,
packs of diapers
bulks of sun cream
extra toys, extra clothes, extra shoes, extra snacks,
when just packing up his mess
at the end of the day
is enough to strain my back.

I wanted to go on holiday with my toddler son
but then I realized I would have to actually plan for each day,
activities, play,
beach, adventures, and other shit advertised for ‘family fun’ in the flyers,
when my gut instinct tells me
those ‘happy moms’ in the brochures
are all just fucking liars.

I wanted to go on holiday with my toddler son
but then I realized each day to my son, is a holiday,
perhaps I’ll wait for him to go to college
then I’ll have my way,
I’d better start packing though- it’s only 16 years away!

375.

I hunt for the toys
with advertisements
that promise;
"your kid will have hours of fun".
But each toy disappoints me
more than the
next one.
Because for each one,
my son,
plays for a few minutes
and then he's done.
So I always end up
writing back
requesting a refund:

Dear Toy Company,

I am disappointed.

This product I bought
did not keep my kid busy
for hours-
you see, I am a mother
using all my super powers;
I cook and clean, and play
and go to the office the next day.
I get a rare hour to myself
once every blue moon,
I'd love it if your toy kept my kid busy,
but he's more interested
in drinking my perfume.

Thus,
I am returning it for a refund,
because I've used up
all my retirement fund
paying for toys, hoping my son enjoys, hoping I'll get an hour without noise.

Now I don't have any money
to go to a nursing home
when I've lost all my health-
and I desperately need to get there,
because it's my only hope,
for time to myself.

Yours sincerely,
Every Mother.

N.B. No, I don't want the refund in a gift card.

376.

I am that mom.

The one who picks up
her kids from school,
wearing yoga pants
breaking all fashion rules.

I am that mom.

The one who buys
the baked goodies from the store
not even pretending
they are home-made.
I am not a cook or a maid.

I am that mom.

Who works
two jobs
and gets paid for one,
because what I do at home
is not seen as worthy of pay.

I am that mom.

With no time for play,
or to fit into your description of ideal.

I am that mom.

And you would be too, if you kept it fucking real.

N.B. To all the judgemental moms in the school parking lot.

377.

Don't ask me
when I'll have more kids,
I haven't been having sex,
lately.

Don't ask me
when I'll have more kids,
I haven't been sleeping much,
lately.

Don't ask me
when I'll have more kids,
because motherhood has been a nightmare
and bliss,
and I am grateful.

Grateful for this experience
of being a mom-
but there's so much in my life
that I still haven't done.

Don't ask me
when I'll have more kids,
instead ask me,
how am I working on my happiness,
lately.

***

"What a shame that
he'll be an only child...a lonely child",

someone said,
when I told them I don't want to have any more children,
and I want to focus on my career, instead.

"No it's not a shame",
I objectively responded to them being sappy-
"being a lonely child,
is better than being one of many,
with a mother who is
extremely unhappy".

N.B. The increased time pressure associated with second births explains mothers' worse mental health. (Source: 2018 research in Journal of Marriage and Family, https://doi.org/10.1111/jomf.12531)

378.

To the woman annoyed at me,
for posting one too many
pictures of my baby
on my social media page,
I just want to say;

I don't get annoyed when you post endlessly,
about your big work promotion
or that project you're working on-
my baby is my achievement,
my job is a mom.

And my job is not less worthy
just because I get no financial pay,
mark my words
for what I'm about to say
is long overdue;
we must show
the same respect,
for all the jobs that women do.

379.

In Eastern culture,
it is a shame
for a woman
to enter any profession
whereby she uses her body
to make her own profit.

Want to be an actress? Shame.
Want to be a model? Shame.
Want to be a fashionista? Shame.
Want to be a sex worker? Shame.

The only acceptable
position, wherein,
a woman is encouraged
to use her body
is that of a wife and/or a mother.

Why?
Because it is just a man
that ends up profiting.

380.

When I was a young girl
I wanted to be a belly dancer.
I practiced dancing in my room
in the mirror
in the memory
of crystal chandeliers
glistening, in a flirtation
with my skin.

I danced in the mirror
and looked at myself-
the way I've seen
men look at belly dancers
while they eat greasy food
with a moustache dipped
in hummus dip
hungry for a sip
from her whiskey
lips,
her scotch tanned,
limbs.

I wanted to be a belly dancer
but my father said no-
he was worried my flesh would be
meat
for men
to eat
to meet
heaven.
A temporary passage

a pit stop, an asylum
for sinners.
That's no way for a woman to live.

I wanted to be a belly dancer
but my father said no-
he was worried about men objectifying me.
Oh father, but you know
that's exactly how any woman's life
turns out to be.

381.

Thigh gap.
Pay gap.
Gender gap.

How many more
gaps
do I need to fill?

***

Pay me
for the work I put on
my desk,
not for what I have under
my dress.

***

Because I am a woman,
for my labour in the workplace
you pay me less.

Why of course, you would-
how can I expect, anything else?

For you were raised
from your mother's unpaid labour-
so me, getting paid at all,
to you, is excess.

382.

I write those words to you,
from jail.
I ask if you know how much
is the bail-
to free me?

I have been locked up
for 32 years,
held captive by,
my warden of tears.
I do not understand what is my crime.

But it seems I'll be locked up for a very long time.
Like the women before me.

I am
in a prison cell,
the size of it, oh well,
never seems to be
good enough.

I am judged for embracing it, for thinking myself tough.

I am
behind the bars
of my chocolate brown
skin,
inside the structure
of a female body-
scrutinized, regulated, controlled
by laws, religions, and basically everybody.

They argue and disagree, on what is right for me.

But if I say I just want to be free, they all get angry.

I am locked up,
trapped
inside a jail
where even my visitors,
my family, my lovers, cannot see,
that I've been locked up
for 32 years,
inside a body, mine-
but not owned by me.

***

You sexualize my body
You regulate my womb.
You make the world a scary place,
so that I'll only be safe
between the walls of my tomb.

You dictate who I can
and cannot love,
you control my career options-
you don't pay me enough.

You control my body
and legislate my life,
to shut me up.
But no matter what you do-
my voice and my soul,

can never be (*will never be*),
controlled by you.

383.

Let me tell you
about the world I belong to,
where women must not shake hands with men
or have painted nails while they pray,
where because our wombs bleed emotions,
men are the rational ones with the final say.

Let me tell you
about the world I belong to,
where women live in the state of prey
hunted by men, seduced by them,
but killed by honour if we reciprocate their play.

Let me tell you
about the world I belong to,
where women are modern day slaves
and by modern I mean
they live with all the money and means
to buy freedom,
but their freedom isn't offered for sale.

Let me tell you
about the world I belong to,
where women think they are free to choose
the cloaks they wear, and to hide their hair
they do not realize,
they have been conditioned to think
that their life is fair.

Let me tell you
about the world I belong to,

where women choose not to fight
it's easier to sit back,
choking on pearls
decorating their throats
as the throb of silk robes,
is robbing their backs.

Let me tell you
about the world I belong to,
where it is so expensive to be me-
I have been living in debt, spending all of my blood and sweat
for the day, I can afford to be free.

384.

They tell me
to check,
what stereotypes
I ate.

They tell me
my words
incite,
Middle Eastern hate.

They tell me
my writing
supports,
a Western debate.

They tell me
the West will hate us more.
If you keep opening, closed doors.

But I don't write
looking for love-
from you, or the West, or the skies above.

I don't want love.

I want freedom.

***

THE 2ND LIST OF SHIT THAT MADE ME A FEMINIST

Farida D.

I don’t use my name when I write
because I was born in a tribe
where women aren’t allowed
to dip the quill
into their blue and black bruises
to write stories
on white paper, for white people
stripping naked from brown traditions-
where a pen
is forbidden
to touch the flesh of a woman.
The only phallic object a woman is allowed to hold
is the husband which her father sold
her to.

I don’t use my name
because it isn’t mine-
because they poured this blood in me
to break my spine
to mould me,
into what I don’t want to be-
another stomped upon sand dune,
in their victorious male history.

385.

"Not all men!"
"Not all religions!"
"All lives matter!"
"Where's the straight parade?!"-
are all rebuttals
loaded with hate,
for the 'other'.

To those I say;

All men exist in a system
that allows them to abuse.

All religions control women,
restricting their freedom to choose.

Not all lives live in a skin
that makes their living a fear.

Every day is a fucking
straight parade, my dear.

When a problem arises,
the right response is to resolve it-
don't silence the oppressed
with your "not all" bullshit.

386.

Let's hand out a gold medal;

To all the men
who take care of their kids
cook dinner
and change a nappy,
who make sure
they do their share of housework
to keep their wives happy.

Let's hand out a gold medal;

To all the men
who make their partner orgasm
before they do
or better yet, offers them a round two.

Let's hand out a gold medal;

To all the men
who never catcall or harass or rape
this sort of 'nice guy'
deserves a Nobel Prize, or at least a date.

Let's hand out a gold medal;

To all the men, who behave like a regular human,
because the bar has been set so low-
so when they treat us good (as they should)
they now expect to be

the stars of the show.

387.

"Women and men,
are equal!!" I cried.

"Does this mean
I can punch you?" he grins
with snide.

"No,
it means
I can punch you!" I replied.

***

Don't tell me
I can't do
what men do.
The only thing
that stops us women
is when we believe,
assholes like you.

388.

Don't call me 'babe'
I'm not your babe.

Don't call me 'sweetheart'
I'm not your sweetheart.

Don't call me 'love'
I'm not your love.

Doesn't it piss you off
too,
when strange men call you,
sweet names?

If you must call me something,
call me 'demon'-
because I'm setting your sexism,
on flames.

***

Does he hold open your door,
and carry your heavy bags
from the grocery store,
because he's a kind person
who does this with everybody
(even with other men)?

Or does he do it because
he thinks a woman's body,
isn't able

to handle,
anything heavy?

Does he do it because he's nice,
and that's the way he treats everybody?

Or does he do it because he thinks as a woman, you can't do it yourself,
because you have a weak body?

N.B. Look out for benevolent sexism.

389.

My father constantly
travelled,
between two worlds.

One was of patriarchy-
it was his first home, the place he was born
they know him so well, they treat him so well.

And the other world was of gender equality-
it was a place he longed after,
after
he had daughters
after
he saw they weren't welcome
in his home.

My father constantly
travelled,
between two worlds,
he was a nomad
who was torn-
and we travelled along with him,
so that...
he won't feel...
alone.

390.

It’s her choice-
she chose a religion
that glorifies men
oppresses women.

But they told her there was no other path
to reach heaven.

It’s her choice-
she chose the short dress
as the way to impress.

But that’s what they taught her
‘be sexy, to be noticed’.

It’s her choice-
she chose a hijab
to hide in a niqab
looking drab.

Because otherwise, she’s told
she'll be up for grabs.

It’s her choice-
she doesn’t want a career
wants a man to call her dear
to bear his children, year after year
to keep his house nice and neat.

Because, otherwise, she's told, she's incomplete.

It's her choice-
she doesn't want to drive a car
doesn't want to travel far
won't stay late at the bar.

Because if she reported her assault
she'd be called bizarre.

The patriarchy is pleased
when a woman is deceived
to choose her own oppression
without question-
so that they can say;
"It's her choice!"
"Hear her voice!"
"We didn't force her!"
"Let's rejoice!"

It's her choice- they say,
but is it *really* her choice?
Did she have any other choice?
Can she walk a different way?

Let me ask you now
honestly, no lies-
what would happen if,
she chose otherwise?

If she ripped off her hijab,
or chose a career?
If she travelled alone,
lived without fear?
“She’s a rebel”, they'll say
“Send her to hell- straightaway”

So in reality she can’t choose
outside what’s already chosen
that is the conclusion-
they make her think she’s made a choice
but her freedom of choice is an illusion,
a carefully choreographed delusion.

391.

What if we prayed
to a Goddess?
Will all the misogynists become
atheists?

392.

Dear God,

Liberate me.

I plead of you
to re-create me.

I don't want to serve
as a slave, a victim
of this soft skin
I'm in,
moulded for the male gaze.

God, re-create me
I beg you to re-imagine me,
in other ways.

I don't want to spend my days
as a subject, an object,
for a man.
I don't want him to treat me,
as a less than.

There is so much more, to who I am.

God, can you please liberate me?

Signed,
Woman

***

Dear Woman,

I did not create you-
to exist,
from his,
point of view.

He did.

And he created me-
in the way that you see
from his imagination, too.

As an excuse, to use, to abuse
in my name,
all that he does, to oppress you.

Woman, can you please not blame me?

Signed,
God

393.

The oppression
of women
is born out of patriarchy-
all other religious and political tools
are merely aligned
to worship
patriarchy.

Our oppressor is not any one religion
or culture or political system-
our oppressor is the patriarchy.

***

The biggest sin of all,
that people often foresee-
is the sin of mortals who forge,
God's identity.

394.

"I don't see you pray"
my mother would judgementally say,
after her rant,
with God is done, she starts with me,
darting her words, accusingly
as she rolls up her prayer matt,
putting it back in the corner
where it often sat,
like a naughty school boy
waiting for her forgiveness
five times a day.

"I pray-
Mother", I told her,
"I pray every day".

I pray,
with raindrops
that bow down
to worship, the brown
of my skin.

I pray,
with lovers
who cleanse their sin,
within,
the temple of my body.

I pray,
with the forgiveness
of a soft jazz, choir-

I recite melody,
that saves my soul from
eternal hellfire.

I pray,
with every chant
from my beating heart,
for the women, who look for permission
to share their art.
For the revolutions, of hope
that did not yet start.

I pray,
just not in the way,
that you do-
only five times a day, reciting a memorized script.
I pray, all the time, every day-
like a virgin,
wishing to strip.

***

Mother, you see,
I am moulded of earth-
the ocean is my temple
and the sand is my sanctuary.

I don't only pray
every day-
I worship, the life,
in every part of me.

395.

Monotheism is a myth.

We worship so many Gods.

There's the God of Materialism, and the God of Consumerism-
Adam is still obsessed with the *Apple*
(except, it's not an actual fruit anymore).

There's the God of Social Media
who rewards believers
with 'follows' and 'likes',
while Satan unleashes his trolls
to cause strikes.

There's the God of Entertainment, the God of Hollywood, and the God of Bollywood-
24/7 our eyes are glued
to their big screens,
the history of humanity has never seen,
such devotion.

We worship all those Gods
with an ostentatious display
of a sacred splurge.
But on Sundays we pretend
that the only God we ever worship
is the God of the Church.

***

Our homes are full,
but our hearts
are still hungry.

Our kitchens have become supermarkets-
full of stuff we don't need
just a reflection of our greed,
bananas waiting to rot, shit we'll never get to eat.

Our closets are the size of department stores-
but we still don't have anything to wear
because nothing goes with
the holes in our souls.

Our living rooms look like the ones in the catalogues-
glossy
chic,
and empty.

Our bedrooms have become hotels-
bedding strangers,
who leave dents in the shape
of their bodies on us
for a while,
but never ever
leave their hearts behind.

What is behind
this consuming need
to have everything
except for the things
that actually matter?

***

Money can't buy happiness
because happiness isn't sold.

396.

"What's your
mother tongue?"
they ask, to know where I belong.

"Arabic" I said,
but before they box me
in a tiny,
neat set,
I told them;

I speak Arabic
I write English
I eat Indian
I drink Irish,
I dress American.

I live Italian,
I dance African
I pray Balinese.

I read Shakespeare
I eat biryani
I drink whiskey
I wear jeans.

I live for slow sweet
moments of nothing.
I dance with my heart
not with my body.
I pray for inner peace
for everybody.

My tongue is Arabic, but my soul...
oh, my soul,
it does not speak in one language that can only be heard,
by a select of people.

My soul, and my spirit- it is not tied to a land,
it soars like a bird.
My soul, and my spirit-
it belongs to the world.

Language, has become like the land
with borders, and walls, and rules to enter and rules to occupy,
to know what's your mother tongue,
where you truly belong
don't ask yourself what language you speak,
ask yourself;
What is the language in which you laugh and which you cry?
What is the language spoken by the soil,
that would be your home when you die?

***

The only race
I belong to,
is human.

397.

Don't tell me
I need to wash my skin
with white
for you to respect me.

This brown I'm in
is from my burning
in hell
and rising, again and again.

***

This race I'm in,
is running out of time
is running out of patience
is running out of fucks
is running out of rationale
to see
why the colour of my skin
is the only thing you notice
when you look at me.

398.

When we talk about them-
they are just women,
but we are 'women of colour'.

They have just bodies,
but we are 'plus-size' or 'skinny'.

When we talk about them-
our choice of words,
makes them the norm
and us, the outcasts of this world.

***

I am not, a Muslim feminist.

I am not, an Arab feminist.

I am not, a Woman of Colour feminist.

I am just, a feminist.

Ironically-
to win this fight of intersectionality,
I must ditch all those labels
because ultimately,
I am fighting for my right to be-
to exist beyond labels, beyond discrimination,
to be defined by me.

399.

Do you know
what it's like
paying mortgage,
to live under skin
you can never own?

400.

We stood
on the tips of our tails,
ready to run-
on your marks! Get set!
the race has begun.

The rules stated that
if you win, you would be given,
your other half to complete you.
And your life will begin, born from a woman,
into a happily ever after-
everyone was pushing ahead,
so I ran even faster.

I was an X, in a race of X's and Y's
but nobody told me that in this run
the winning position, is actually only ever given,
to a Y.
If an X would win, she'll still be given skin,
but she'll wear shame, till she dies.

I left a good place,
to come into this world
and I don't mean this to be sarcasm-
but I should I have stayed where I was
for I was happier living,
as an orgasm.

To the one not yet born:
Unlearn...

Unlearn all the shit!

Made in the USA
Middletown, DE
18 December 2020

28744057R00187